Nick's Creative Cooking Made Easy

by Nick Ligidakis

with special introduction by Brad Steiger

ISBN: 0-9615418-4-9

First Printing – January, 1987

Second Printing – July, 1988

Third Printing – December, 1991

Fourth Printing – March, 1997

Editorial supervision by Brad Steiger
Photographs by David Putnam
Typography and book production by Tommy Kay

Printed in the United States of America.

Other works by Nick Ligidakis . . .

"My Golden Collection of Original Desserts"
© 1993

"5024 E. McDowell"
A Man's Journey Into Culinary Exploration
© 1997

Coming Soon . . .

"The Heros Of My Thoughts"

Contact Above Address To Order.

Thank You

I dedicate this book to my parents, Anatasia and Stefanos, the two best people who ever walked on this Earth.

Nick Ligidakis —
From Soccer Star
to Creative Chef

Nick Ligidakis is an award-winning restauranteur who is fast becoming known as the "People's Chef." There is no question that with his creative and unorthodox culinary techniques he is making a bold mark in the cooking world.

Born Nicolaos Stefanos Ligidakis on Christmas Day, 1945, in the small town of Kiaton, Korinthias, Greece, his transformation of the **Golden Cuisine** into a gourmet's paradise is a genuine, old-fashioned American success story.

Approach the **Golden Cuisine** on any night other than Monday — Nick's one day of rest — and you will observe men and women standing patiently outside, waiting to be served. If you, too, are standing in line, chatting pleasantly with the other good folks around you, you will discover that you are visiting with people who have driven from as far away as Texas to eat a meal prepared by the smiling, self-voiced Greek.

What is Nick's secret? Why would dozens of men and women drive for hours for the singular privilege of waiting their turn to sit a **Golden Cuisine** table?

"I make everything for each meal after the order has been placed," Nick responds. "Nothing is processed or waiting in the refrigerator. And every one of my recipes is original. I have created each one of them."

Nick continues, freely sharing his thoughts on creative cooking:

"I have been called a 'Master Chef', a 'Philosopher of Cooks', and the the 'People's Chef. All of this attention would be good for my ego if I were into that sort of thing.

"I do like to be called the 'People's Chef', though, because I really do cook for people.

"I try always to do my best in my work, because I love my work. I like to be unique; but, yet, I like to be simple. I don't like to give a dish a fancy name so that I can give your wallet indigestion.

I *am* a people's chef. I don't like to wear the high hat and the squeaky clean white uniform that would give me the image of having come from a different world. I don't want to talk about complicated cooking techniques and culinary terms in order to impress people. I only want to impress people with my cooking.

"I like to cook plain foods in a different and rich manner. I like to stand at the stove in my jeans and to be myself.

"Once an elderly lady complained that my jeans were full of flour. I answered, 'Dear lady, my jeans are full of flour because I am a cook. If I were a surgeon, my jeans would be full of blood.'"

Interestingly, Nick Ligidakis came to this country as a professional athlete, not as a master chef from the Greek Islands.

As a young boy, he had but one love: soccer. And as he became more proficient at the sport, it seemed clear that the fastest road to fame and fortune for Nikos would lie in his magic feet and his endurance.

An ankle injury slowed down what would have been a most promising career in soccer, but he continued to play the sport. He graduated from college with an engineering degree, but he had little interest in pursuing such work.

He looked with great affection at his mother, Anatasia, his father Stefanos, his brothers Lefteris, Andreas, Giorgos, and his sister Sophia. Life was good for them in Greece, but Nick yearned to be a world traveler.

It was at that time that some big-time operators approached the restless young man. They had the idea of bringing a group of Greek All-Stars to the States and matching them against some American soccer teams. It was their plan to set up an extensive tour of American cities and to cash in on the growing interest in soccer in the United States.

Nick was offered a salary that made his heart beat faster. This was a fantastic opportunity. After a few months playing soccer in the States, he could save himself a nice nest egg and return to Greece a prosperous man.

It seemed a really fine plan. An excellent opportunity. But then the big-time promoters ran out of money a few weeks after practice had begun. The young Greek athletes were stranded in Chicago.

Most of Nick's desperate teammates wired home to Greece for money to fly back to familiar soccer fields, but the enterprising Ligidakis decided to test the Great American Dream Machine for himself.

"I never stop," Nick states firmly. "I never give up. As a Greek, I believe in the indomitable human spirit. As an American, I believe in the free enterprise system and democracy in action. Please remember also that democracy in action. Please remember also that democracy was born in Greece."
ed a nightclub, got married, then moved to Arizona.

Then things started to go bad. He separated from his wife, but maintained his responsibility to her and to his kids — Lisa Nicole, Steven Michael, Joseph Nicholas. The bad luck stretched into a mean run, and Nick was broke again.

Somehow, a small restaurant caught his attention. Its owners, a married couple, wanted to sell.

Nick had no more than pocket change, but he walked into the place and told the man and his wife that he would pay them the price that they were asking. He assured them that he was a honest, hard-working man and that he would make good the money if they would give him a chance to make payments.

When the couple responded to Nick's sincere and earnest manner by accepting his terms, he literally moved into the restaurant and began to make it his total universe.

"I had no other place to stay," he laughs at the memory. "I had no apartment, no car. But now I had the **Golden Cuisine.** I slept on an air mattress in the back. I worked from eight in the morning until two the next morning, seven days a week — for 18 months without a single day off!"

Commitment. Discipline. Hard work. It paid off.

Once you have savored the masterful Southern European cooking — whether you have eaten a complete meal, ordered one of those incredible pizzas or had one of those delicious submarine sandwiches — you have tasted the distinctive difference that makes Nick's place so much more than a restaurant.

The **Golden Cuisine** has become a way of life for thousands of satisfied customers. Surely, there are such masterworks as the

Chicken Plaka, the **Fettucini Formaggi,** the **Coconut Fried Shrimp;** but the essential element that truly makes the restaurant work is the warm, friendly personality of Nick Ligidakis that permeates every nook and cranny of the place. More than one customer has commented about the phenomenon that hs Nick treating him or her like an old friend from the very first time of their meeting.

And here are a few more revealing comments from your friend, Nick Ligidakis:

From Greek soccer fields to his triumph over apparent defeat and understandable despair, Nick has carved his own niche in the annals of American success stories.

And with success comes offers ot opportunities tor "big-time bucks.":

"Representatives of supermarket chains have approached me about marketing my products," Nick states. "The problem is that they will do so only if I consent to have preservatives added to my ingredients. I have turned them down, for I have pride in my work.

"Big investors have begun to walk into the *Golden Cuisine,* wanting to open fancy places where they can become my partners. I have turned them away, because I care more for the people who have truly helped me to grow."

As an additional gift to those devoted customers who have helped him to grow — and to all devotees of superb cooking — Nick now offers this book, a marvelous guide to creative cooking.

"In this book, I am not going to bore you with recipes that have been set down over and over again. Neither am I going to provide you with basic information. I can't teach you how to cook. All I can do is share my original recipes with you. From that point on, you are on your own. You must develop your own style and technique of cooking.

"The simple truth about cooking is this: Take pride in your work and use the best ingredients available. Use your own judgments about changing, adding, or substituting ingredients.

"If you don't love to cook, don't even bother to read my book, because all these recipes have been assembled with a lot of hard work and a great deal of pride."

I hope that you all accept the invitation to join Nick Ligidakis in his adventures in creative cooking. And don't be intimidated. Remember that Nick the master chef was once a professional athlete who could barely prepare scrambled eggs and toast. Commitment and application of effort will pay off everytime!

Brad Steiger, author of
Valentino, Judy Garland, Thorpe's Gold

1

Appetizers and Creations

Every one of my fried appetizers is dipped in buttermilk pancake mix, prepared as follows:

2 cups Buttermilk Pancake Mix
3 cups of water
Mix well with a wire whip.

"The cooking of Nick Ligidakis at the Golden Cuisine is a delight that I can always count on when I'm looking for an appetizing lunch, a zesty pizza extravaganza or when I'm looking for a nice place to share a meal with a date.
"His Italian culinary arts make living in the Valley of the Sun gastronimcally worthwhile."
Suzanne R. DeWeese
Arizona State University
School of Music

Fried Zucchini

2 medium size zucchini,
  cut into 1/4" slices
Flour
4 cups bread crumbs
1 Tbsp. parsley flakes

Buttermilk pancake mix
  (See page 1)
1 tsp. granulated garlic
1 tsp. black pepper

Dip zucchini in pancake batter, coat with flour, and dip back into the buttermilk batter. Mix the breadcrumbs, parsley flakes, garlic and black pepper well, and coat the zucchini thoroughly on all sides.

Oil for deep frying, heat to 375°

Add a few zucchini at a time, frying until golden brown.

Grated Parmesan or Romano cheese

Sprinkle the cheese over the fried zucchini. Serve with Ranch Style dressing. Makes 4 servings.

> *"Nick Ligidakis — one of the best culinary artists in the nation. Nick is a man who cooks with energy and love . . .*
> *"A true Chef of the Gods."*
>   **Joe Higdon**
>   **Phoenix, Arizona**

Deep Fried Mushrooms

1 lb. of medium
  sized mushrooms

Flour
Bread crumbs

Dip mushrooms in buttermilk mix (see page 1). Then coat mushrooms in flour and dip them back into the buttermilk mix. Then, coat the mushrooms with bread crumbs.

Oil for deep frying, heat to 375°

Fry until golden brown. Serve with Ranch Style dressing as a dip. Makes 3 to 4 servings.

"Once you taste Nick's magnificient creation, you'll probably start having dreams craving big Stuffed Rice Balls.
"With hot, melted cheese inside — they're almost as good as dreams about . . . you know what I mean!"

Zan Taylor
Systems Consultant
The Video Bench, Inc.

Fried Rice Balls

2 cups rice   1 qt. chicken stock

Combine in a saucepan, bring to boil until all liquid is absorbed, about 20 minutes.

1/4 cup grated Parmesan   3 Tbsp. unsalted butter
1/4 cup grated Romano   Pepper, to taste

Add to the rice. Cool at room temperature. When cool, roll rice into balls about 3-inches in diameter.

8 oz. of shredded Mozzarella cheese

Form cheese into smaller balls, about 1-inch round.

Place a Rice Ball in the palm of your hand. Insert the cheese into the center of the Rice Ball.

2 eggs, beaten   3 cups dry breadcrumbs

Roll balls in beaten eggs to coat well. Then roll balls in dry breadcrumbs to seal well.

Oil for frying, heat to 375°

Fry until golden brown. When done, sprinkle with grated Romano cheese.

Broccoli Melt

10 Broccoli flowerets, parboiled
1 lb. of yellow or white cheddar cheese, shredded

1 Tbsp. milk
Flour
Dry bread crumbs
Grated Romano cheese

Divide cheese into 10 parts, and coat each broccoli floweret with cheese. Dip each broccoli ball into the Buttermilk Pancake Mix (page 1)., coat balls with flour, and dip them back into the batter.

Roll the broccoli balls in the dry bread crumbs, coating each thoroughly.

Oil for frying, heat to 400°

Fry until golden brown. Serve with Ranch Dressing or tomato sauce.

Fried Bay Shrimp

1 lb. of tiny Bay Shrimp
Flour

Buttermilk Pancake Mix (see page 1)

Dip Shrimp in pancake batter, then coat with flour.

Oil for frying, heat to 400°.

Fry until golden brown. Serve with cocktail sauce.

"**Nick's** Golden Cuisine **is literally an oasis in the desert. In this part of the country most of the eateries are indictintive of each other as far as creativity in their menu is concerned.**

"**Nick brings an refreshing ethnic flavor in quality and reasonably priced dining. Whenever we have visitors from back east, I always recommend this establishment because I know they'll not be disappointed. Keep up the good food!**"
Vince Adselno
Tempe, Arizona

"There are not enough superlatives to describe the sumptuous experience that is dining with Nick and Karen at Golden Cuisine. *Every dish is a unique creation prepared by a master of the culinary arts with the innate sense of putting you at home within a truly welcoming atmosphere.*

"*Amid an array of delectable appetizers, calzones, entree's, etc. are Nick's sinfully delicious desserts. What do I recommend? Everything on the menu! My favorites —* Fried Mozzarella Stocks, Classic Greek pizza, lasagne il re . . .

"*Be ready for the treat of your life when eating at Nick's.*"

Alice Wiley-Proski

Fried Mozzarella Sticks

1 lb. Mozzarella cheese, cut into 1" x 1" x 4" rectangles
Dry bread crumbs

Buttermilk Pancake Mix (see page 1).
Flour

Dip Mozzarella sticks in pancake batter, coat with flour and dip back into the buttermilk batter. Roll the sticks in the dry bread crumbs, making sure each is coated well on all sides.

Oil for frying, heat to 400°

Fry until golden brown. Serve with tomato sauce.

Asparagus Spears

8 Asparagus Spears
4 thin slices of cheddar
  cheese
1 Tbsp. flour

4 thin slices of cooked ham
2 eggs, separated
Dry bread crumbs

Trim and peel the 8 asparagus spears. Parboil for about 2 minutes and drain. Lay out the 4 slices of ham, place a thin slice of cheddar cheese on top of each piece of ham. Place two asparagus spears on top of each ham/cheese stack, and wrap tightly into rolls.

Separate the egg whites and yolks, and beat each well. Then fold the yolks into the beaten egg white. Fold the flour into the eggs. Dip the asparagus rolls into the egg mixture, then coat each roll thoroughly with the bread crumbs.

Oil for deep frying, heat to 375°

Fry until golden brown. Serve with mustard sauce.

Stuffed Onions

3 Large sweet onions
1 Tbsp. chopped onion pulp
1-1/2 cups dry bread crumbs
3 Tbsp. chopped parsley
1 Clove of garlic, chopped

1/2 tsp. Oregano
1 Tbsp. lemon juice
1 Tbsp. butter
2 Tbsp. grated Romano
  cheese

Peel the onions and cut in half, crosswise. Simmer in water for about 20 minutes. Remove the center portions to create a hollow. Combine the chopped onion pulp, bread crumbs, parsley, garlic, oregano and lemon juice, mixing well. Spoon this mixture into the center of the onions.

Drizzle the melted butter over the top of the onions, and sprinkle with the grated Romano cheese. Cover and bake at 325°, for about 30 minutes. Serve at room temperature. Makes 4 to 6 servings.

Eggplant Ripieri

4 slices of a medium
  eggplant, 1/4" thick
Flour
Dry bread crumbs

8 slices of Provolone cheese
8 slices of Mortadella
Buttermilk pancake mix
  (see page 1)

Place one slice of Mortadella, topped with a slice of Provolone, then a slice of eggplant, and then top with Provolone and Mortadella. Make 4 stacks.

Dip each stack in pancake batter, then coat with flour and dip back into the buttermilk mix. Finally, coat the eggplants well with dry breadcrumbs.

Oil for frying, heat to 375°.

Fry until golden brown. Serve with tomato sauce.

Escargot

1 lb. butter
1/4 cup chopped garlic
1 tsp. Worchestshire sauce
2 drops hot pepper sauce
3 dz. canned snails, drained

1/2 cup chopped parsley
2 Tbsp. chopped scallions
2 Tbsp. red wine
1 tsp. lemon juice

Place butter in a bowl and mix until soft. Add al the other ingredients except the snails to the butter, and mix well.

Place the drained snails in shells and fill with a generous amount of the butter mixture. Place in baking dish.

Bake in oven at 400°, about 8 minutes, until all of the butter mix is melted.

"Nick makes everyday food become a Gourmet's Delight.
"He's terrific!"
    Henry Dailey
    Phoenix, Arizona

Brochettes of Snails

3/4 cup butter
2 extra Tbsps. butter
3-1/2 Tbsp. chopped shallots
2 Tbsp. chopped green
  onions
1-1/4 cup white wine

3/4 cup whipping cream
1 Tbsp. minced garlic
Dash of pepper
Dry bread crumbs
2 dz. snails

Melt 3/4 cup of butter in a saucepan. Add 3 tablespoons of chopped shallots and saute until soft. Add the snails and 3/4 cup of the white wine. Simmer for 20 minutes, until tender.

Add whipping cream, stir well. Then remove from heat.

Add minced garlic, pepper and green onions to the sauce, and then the cool snails, being sure to coat each snail completely with the sauce.

Thread the snails onto wooden skewers, and roll in the bread crumbs. Broil the snail skewers until light brown.

Meantime, saute 1/2 tablespoons of the chopped shallots in a tablespoon of butter. Add the last 1/2 cup of white wine and the final tablespoon of butter. Remove this sauce from heat and place on a serving plate. Place the broiled snail skewers on top, and serve.

Stuffed Zucchini Flowers

1/2 cup spinach leaves, chopped
1/2 cup cabbage leaves chopped
1/2 cup mushrooms, thinly sliced
1/2 stalk celery, chopped
1 small carrot, chopped
1/4 tsp. Pepper
1 Tbsp. chopped onions

3 Tbsp. vegetable oil
1 Tbsp. mint leaves
2 cloves garlic, chopped
Zucchini flowers
1-1/3 cup buttermilk
  pancake mix
1 cup beer

Heat two tablespoons of the cooking oil in a large saucepan and add all vegetables, cooking until wilted. Add mint leaves, garlic and pepper. Rinse the zucchini flowers in water and stuff them with the vegetable mixture.

Mix well the buttermilk pancake mix and beer. Dip the zucchini flowers in this flour mixture and coat well. Heat oil for deep frying to 325°, and fry until golden brown.

Feta Leaves

6 large grapevine leaves
6 oz. soft Feta cheese,
  crumbled

2 oz. chopped sun dried
  tomatoes
3 Tbsps. olive oil

Place 1 piece of Feta cheese, 2 tomatoes and 1/2 tablespoon of olive oil on each grapeleaf. Fold the leaves to enclose the contents.

Grill until soft, or about 10 minutes.

Open the grapeleaves and scoop out the cooked filling. Then serve with toasted French bread.

Asparagus in Filo

1/2 cup butter
2 Lbs. asparagus,
  cut into 1/2 pieces
1 cup grated Swiss cheese
4 Tbsps. chopped garlic
16 sheets of Filo dough

5 eggs
1/2 lb. Riccota cheese
Pepper, to taste
1/8 cup grated Parmesan
1/2 cup slivered almonds

Heat the butter in a skillet and add asparagus, garlic and slivered almonds. Saute until crisp and tender.

Beat the 5 eggs well in a separate bowl. Add the Riccota, grated Swiss cheese and Parmesan and pepper, then pour the contents of the bowl into the sauteed asparagus.

Brush a 13" x 9" baking dish with melted butter. Lay 1/2 of the Filo on the bottom of the pan, brushing each layer with butter. Fill the dish wtih the asparagus mixture.

Top with the rest of the Filo, brushing each layer. Tack any excess Filo in at the sides of the pan. Make 4 crosswise and 3 lengthwise slits in the dough.

Bake at 350°, 50 to 60 minutes, or until golden brown.

Cheese Triangles

3/4 lb. Feta cheese
1/4 lb. Riccota cheese
3 eggs, beaten
1 lb. Filo dough

1 cup grated Parmesan
2 Tbsps. chopped parsley
2 Tbsps. melted butter
1 Tbsp. nutmeg

Mix the cheeses, eggs and melted butter thoroughy. Cut each sheet of Filo into strips about 4-inches wide. Working on the Filo at the same time as you are mixing the cheese.

Brush each strip with a bit of melted butter. Place 2 teaspoons of the cheese mixture at the bottom of each strip. Fold the corner up to form a triangle. Continue folding dough into a triangular shape.

Place the triangles on a cooking sheet, and brush tops with butter and sprinkle with nutmeg.

Bake at 350°, 20-25 minutes, until light golden brown. Makes about 70 pieces.

Spinach Triangles

3 lbs. spinach, chopped
   and parboiled
10 green onions, chopped
1 Tbsp. chopped dill
1/4 cup parsley, chopped
1/2 cup grated Parmesan

1/8 lb. Riccota cheese
3/4 lb. Feta cheese
6 eggs, beaten
1 lb. Filo dough
Melted butter
1 Tbsp. nutmeg

Follow the same steps for cooking as described in the above recipe for the Cheese Triangles.

These triangle recipes are also excellent fried in olive oil.

"Dear Nick,
   "Your food is wonderful. Your recipes are both delightful and creative. Definitely 'love at first taste!'"

Sincerely yours,
Cheri Skiba
Phoenix, Arizona

Fish Roe Salad

8 oz. fish roe (Tarama)	2 Tbsps. grated onion
1 cup fresh mashed potatoes	3/4 cup olive oil
1 cup of white bread, soaked in water and squeezed dry	Juice of 2 lemons

Place the fish roe in a blender and mix at low speed until creamy. Add the mashed potatoes, the bread, and onion. Then very slowly add the 3/4 cup olive oil and lemon juice while the blender is turning slowly. Cover blender again and mix until light and creamy.

Avocado Tarama

Follow the Fish Roe recipe as give above. Add 2 avocados, peeled and chopped, along with the potatoes.

"European cooking at its best, served here in the good ole U.S.A."

Mannie Ryder
Phoenix, Arizona

Fried Onion Hearts

3 medium sweet red onions, peeled and cut into 1/2" slices.

Take out the center of the slices. Dip rings into the buttermilk pancake mix, described on page 1. Then dip rings in a well-mixed bowl of 1 cup corn meal, 1 cup Matzo meal, 2 cups of flour, and 1/2 cup breadcrumbs. Coat each ring thoroughly, and then dip back into the pancake batter.

Oil for deep frying, heat to 400°

Fry until golden brown. Makes 3 to 4 servings.

Fried Artichoke Hearts

2 cans of artichoke hearts,   Flour
  packed in water, drained   Bread crumbs
Buttermilk Pancake mix   Grated Parmesan cheese
  (see page 1)

Dip artichokes in buttermilk batter, coat with flour and dip back again in the pancake mix. Coat with bread crumbs.

Oil for deep frying, heat to 375°. Fry until golden brown.

Sprinkle with grated Parmesan cheese, and serve with Ranch style dressing.

> *"Your food is tasty, irresistable, and filling. And the most tempting appetizer is Pepperoni Tirato."*
>
> **Mary Curtin**
> **Phoenix, Arizona**

Pepperoni Tirato

2 long marinated red   Buttermilk pancake mix
  peppers   (see page 1)
1 cooked Italian sausage,   3/4 cup Riccota cheese
  sliced thinly   1/8 cup grated Romano
1/2 cup shredded Mozzarella   cheese
  cheese   Flour
Bread crumbs

Mix cheeses and sausage thoroughly. Split peppers lengthwise. Place half of the cheese mixture on each of the peppers. Roll the peppers closed and dip in pancake mix. Coat peppers well with flour and dip again into buttermilk batter. Then roll peppers in bread crumbs, being sure to coat each well.

Oil for deep frying, heat to 375°. Fry until golden brown. Serve with tomato sauce.

"Great food!!!
"We love the atmosphere and personal atten-
tion. The best Garlic Toast *we have EVER*
eaten!"

Thanks,
Dale & Becky
Phoenix, AZ

Garlic Toast

1 loaf of Italian or French bread, sliced into 1-inch thick slices.

SPREAD:

1 cup butter or margarine
2 Tbsps. grated Parmesan
cheese
2 Tbsps. grated Romano
cheese

1/2 cup mayonnaise
4 cloves chopped garlic
3 Tbsps. parlsey flakes

Coat top side of each slice of bread with the thoroughly mixed spread. Bake in a 350° oven for about 8 to 10 minutes, until brown.

Onion Rings

2 large peeled onions
Flour
1/2 cup bread crumbs
1 cup cracker meal

Buttermilk pancake mix
(see page 1)
1 cup cornmeal
1 cup Matzo meal

Slice onions about 1/2-inch thick. Separate into rings. Dip rings into buttermilk batter, coat well with flour and repeat the dipping into the pancake mix.

Thoroughly mix two cups of flour, bread crumbs, corn meal, Matzo meal and cracker meal. Coat each onion ring with this mix.

Oil for deep frying, heat to 400°. Fry until golden brown. Makes 4 to 5 servings.

Shrimp Balls

6 oz. baby shrimp
6 oz. pineapple tidbits
8 oz. shredded Mozzarella
8 oz. shredded coconut

Buttermilk pancake mix
  (see page 1)
Flour

Mix shrimp, pineapple and Mozzarella together. Divide into firmly pressed balls, about 1-inch in diameter. Dip balls in buttermilk batter, coat with flour and dip back into the pancake mix.

Roll the balls into the shredded coconut, covering well.

Oil for frying, heat to 350°. Fry until golden brown. Serve with cocktail sauce.

Chicken Fritters

1-1/2 cups cooked chicken
  cubed
1 cup Swiss cheese, cubed
3 green onions, chopped
1/2 cup heavy mayonnaise
1 tsp. celery seeds

1/2 tsp. pepper
1 cup flour
2 eggs
1/4 cup milk
1 Tbsp. vegetable oil
1 tsp. baking powder

Combine the chicken, cheese and onions. In a separate bowl, mix the other ingredients. Then combine with the chicken mixture.

Oil for frying, heat to 375°. Drop mixture in by the teaspoon. Fry until golden brown.

SAUCE:

1 cup mayonnaise
1-1/2 Tbsps. Dijon mustard

1-1/2 Tbsps. horseradish

Mix well. Use as a cocktail dip for your Chicken Fritters.

2 *Soups*

Vegetable Broth

2 leeks, thinly sliced
2 med. onions, thinly sliced
1 head lettuce, chopped
  into thin slices
6 mushrooms, chopped
1 tsp. thyme
1-1/2 quarts water

2 ribs chopped celery
3 chopped carrots
2 sliced cabbage leaves
4 sprigs parsley, chopped
2 bay leaves
Pepper, to taste

Simmer all in a stew or soup pot for about 1 hour. Makes 1-1/2 quarts.

Chicken Broth

6 to 7 large chicken
  parts
1 garlic bulb, unpeeled
4 whole cloves
5 quarts water

1 large onion
2 carrots
Pepper, to taste
6 mushrooms

Simmer for about 2-1/2 hours. Makes 4 quarts.

"These days, the word 'gourmet' has become a household word for just about everything. I define gourmet as 'The art of cooking that employs a proven recipe, attentive pride, and proper portioning to enhance a food's flavor to its finest level possible'.
"This is also how I describe the talent of Nick Ligidakis."
                    Jeffrey A. Robertson

Beef Broth

2 lbs. beef shanks	5 quarts water
2 lbs. beef short ribs	5 carrots
2 lbs. chicken pieces	1 onion
1 veal shank	1 garlic bulb
Pepper, to taste	

Mix in stew pot. Simmer for about 5 hours. Makes 4 quarts.

Fish Broth

2 lbs. fresh bones and heads, trimmings rinsed, broken into pieces	1 onion, sliced
	1 carrot, sliced
	1 leek, sliced
	1 rib celery, diced
2 quarts water	

Mix and simmer for about 1 hour. Makes 1-1/2 quarts of delicious Fish Broth.

Egg Lemon Soup

9 cups chicken stock	3 large egg yolks
1/4 lb. chicken parts	3 large egg whites
1/2 cup long grain rice	1/4 cup fresh-squeezed lemon juice

Boil chicken stock and parts for 20-25 minutes. Remove chicken. Let cool at room temperature. Discard bones and cut chicken into small parts.

Add rice to the stock and cover. Let cook over medium heat about 15 minutes. Separate the eggs and beat both the yolks and whites well. Add whites to the yolks while continuing to beat thoroughly. Add one cup of the chicken broth to the egg mixture and again beat well. Whisk this egg batter into the chicken stock, blending well.

Makes 6 servings.

Lamb Broth

4 Lamb shanks	2 carrots
3 bay leaves	Pepper, to taste
3 med. onions, sliced	2 half lemons
5 celery branches	Water to cover

Place in stew pot and simmer for about 2 hours.

> *"Being a connoisseur of fine foods and dining, I look to each experience as an adventure. Knowing Nick, and the fine food he serves at the "Golden Cuisine," this recipe book is sure to become my most revered.*
>
> *"Asalute, Nick! To the extension of an already pleasing adventure!"*
>
> Sincerely,
> Glen

Spinach Garlic Soup

4 cups chicken broth	1/2 cup butter
1 lg. head spinach, chopped	8 cloves garlic, chopped
1 lg. carrot, grated	1 lg. onion, chopped
1/2 cup whipping cream	1/4 cup flour
1/2 cup half and half	Pepper, to taste

Add spinach and carrot to chicken broth and cook for about 10 minutes. Remove from heat.

Place butter in a skillet and saute the garlic, onion and a dash of pepper over low heat for about 15-20 minutes. Then add the flour, cooking and stirring for an additional five minutes.

Combine the spinach and onion mixtures, and puree in a blender. Place the contents of the blender into a clean pot.

Add the whipping cream, half and half and pepper to the pureed soup, heating until hot but not allowing to come to a boil.

When serving, garnish each bowl with a dollop of sour cream.

Cauliflower Roquefort Soup

1/2 cup sweet butter	6 cups chicken broth
2 cloves garlic, minced	1 cup half and half
1 shallot, minced	2 oz. Roquefort cheese
1 head cabbage, chopped	2 Tbsps. Vermouth
1 med. cauliflower, chopped	White pepper

Melt the butter in a 4-quart saucepan. Add the garlic, shallot and chopped cabbage and saute for 5 minutes. Then add the cauliflower and chicken broth, covver, and simmer for 25 minutes.

While this mixture is cooking, puree the half and half and the Roquefort cheese in a blender. Add to the soup.

Stir in the Vermouth and white pepper.

Makes 4-6 servings.

Potato Spinach

6 med. potatoes, cleaned and sliced	1 pint half and half
	Dash of pepper
10 oz. spinach	2 tsp. grated nutmeg
1 Tbsp. sweet butter	2 Tbsps. grated Parmesan
2 cloves garlic, minced	10 oz. chicken broth

Cook the potatoes for about 20 minutes. Drain and puree in a blender until smooth. Cook the spinach until soft, drain and chop into small pieces.

Saute the garlic with butter in a large saucepan until the garlic is soft. Add the chicken broth, then the potatoes and spinach. Heat on a low fire, but do not boil.

Add the half and half and stir well. Still stirring, add the pepper, nutmeg and grated Parmesan.

Makes 6 servings.

Garden Soup

1/2 lb. salt pork, diced
1/4 cup olive oil
3 med. onions, chopped
3 cloves garlic, minced
4 med. ribs celery, chopped
4 med. carrots, chopped
1 med. green pepper, chopped
1 cup small pasta shells
4 med. zucchini, sliced thick
2 cups shredded fresh spinach

8 cups chicken broth
2 bay leaves
4 cups cooked white beans
1 tsp. rosemary
1/2 cup minced parsley
1 lbs. sweet Italian sausage cooked, sliced thick
Pesto sauce
Pepper, to taste
Grated jack cheese

Saute salt pork in a kettle, until brown. Drain pot. Add the olive oil, onions and garlic and cook until onions are limp.

Add the celery, carrots and green pepper, stirring in well. Then put the chicken broth, bay leaves, white beans, rosemary and parsley in the pot. Bring to a boil, then reduce heat and simmer for about 10 minutes.

Then add the Italian sausage, pasta shells, zucchini and spinach. Again bring to boil, then reduce heat and simmer for 10 minutes, or until pasta is tender.

Just before serving stir in the Pesto sauce and pepper. On top of each serving, sprinkle a bit of grated jack cheese.

"Consistently delicious meals; creative original recipes; always enough food for an entire crowd on one plate!
"Every visit to Nick & Karen's is extremely pleasing to the palate and a delight to the soul."

Tom and Mica Villaire

Red Pepper Soup

2 Tbsps. minced green onions
4 oz. sweet butter
4 Red bell peppers, chopped

2 cups chicken broth
1 cup whipping cream
Pepper, to taste
Minced parsley

Saute onions, butter and bell peppers over medium heat for about three minutes. Then add the chicken broth, lower the heat and simmer for 15 minutes.

Remove from stove and puree in a blender until the mixture is smooth. Stir in whipping cream, blend well, and then heat. Stir in pepper to taste. Sprinkle the minced parsley on top when serving. Makes 3-4 servings.

Baked Provolone Soup

3 Tbsps. butter, melted
3 Tbsps. flour
1/2 tsp. Dijon mustard
1-1/2 cups shredded Provolone cheese

2 cups chicken broth
10 oz. chopped spinach
1/2 cup shredded carrots
2-1/2 cups milk
1/2 cup finely chopped onions

Blend butter, flour and Dijon mustard over low heat and remove from stove. Stir in chicken broth, then place back on burner and heat to boil, stirring constantly.

Add the spinach, carrots and onions. Reduce heat and cook until the vegetables are soft. Stir in the milk, heat gently, and remove from heat.

Pour soup into individual serving cups and sprinkle the Provolone cheese over the soup. Heat until the cheese is melted. Makes 4-5 servings.

Baked Cabbage Soup

12 large cabbage leaves	1 qt. beef stock
1/4 lb. Pancetta, cubed	Ground nutmeg
6 slices Italian or French bread, sliced 1/2" thick	Ground black pepper
	3/4 stick butter
6 slices Proscuitto, thinly sliced	1/4 lb. Fontina cheese thinly sliced

Blanche cabbage leaves in boiling water. In separate pan, saute the pancetta until barely cooked. Then place the Pancetta in cups, cover with cabbage leaves. Top the cabbage leaves with slices of bread, top the bread with the thinly sliced Proscuitto and then a layer of the Fontina cheese. Add enough beef stock to each cup to cover.

Sprinkle the top with ground nutmeg and ground pepper, and top each cup with a little butter.

Bake in 400° oven for about 30 minutes. Makes 4-5 servings.

Baked Vegetable Soup

1/2 cup melted butter	2 slices bacon
1/3 cup sliced carrots	1/3 cup sliced celery
1/2 cup chopped onions	1 cup diced chicken
1/4 cup sliced mushrooms	Pepper, to taste
1/4 lb. grated Swiss cheese	1/4 cup flour
Grated Parmesan cheese	1 pint chicken stock

Melt butter in a heavy saucepan and saute bacon, celery, carrots, onions, chicken, pepper and mushrooms until all the vegetables are tender. Stir in the flour, until smooth. Gradually add chicken stock, stirring until smooth. Heat over low heat until mixture comes to a boil. Pour into individual serving cups or baking dishes.

Sprinkle grated Swiss cheese and Parmesan on top. Bake in 400° oven, until cheese is melted.

Makes 2-3 servings.

Baked Eggplant Soup

4 small eggplants, peeled,
cut into 1/2" slices
1 quart chicken stock
1 pint whipping cream
1/2 lbs. shredded Mozzarella
cheese

1/2 cup olive oil
7 cloves minced garlic
1 Tbsp. whole thyme
1 lb. sweet red peppers
Pepper, to taste

Saute eggplant for about 3-4 minutes in the olive oil. Add the garlic, then the chicken stock and thyme. Heat to a boil.

Separately, grill the red peppers until the skin blackens. Rub the peppers over water to remove the skin.

Place everything in a blender and puree. Add the whipping cream and pepper to the mixture, then stir and heat gently.

Place in cups. Top soup with shredded Mozzarella cheese and heat in oven until melted. Makes about 6 servings.

Bean Soup

1 lb. white beans
1 finely chopped onion
1 can (8 oz.) tomato sauce
1 Tbsp. parsley, chopped
2 cups beef stock
Pepper, to taste
2 carrots, chopped finely

1 cup chopped celery
2 garlic cloves, chopped
3 bay leaves
1 tsp. mint
1/2 cup olive oil
1/2 tsp. thyme

Soak beans in water overnight.

Saute carrots, celery, onion, garlic, bay leaves, mint, thyme and parsley in olive oil in a heavy pot, cooking until vegetables are soft. Add the tomato sauce, pepper and beef stock, stirring thoroughly. Add the beans and enough water to cover. Simmer for about 1 hour. Makes 2-3 servings.

Lentil Soup

1 lb. lentils	1/4 cup red wine vinegar
1/4 cup olive oil	1/4 cup red wine
2 onions, chopped	1 tsp. oregano
3 celery branches, chopped	Pepper, to taste
3 carrots, chopped	3 Tbsps. tomato puree
2 cloves garlic, minced	1 Tbsp. Worchestershire sauce
3 bay leaves	

Soak the lentils overnight. On cooking day, saute the onions, celery, carrots, garlic and bay leaves in olive oil in a heavy soup pot until soft.

Add the vinegar, red wine, oregano, pepper, tomato puree and Worchestershire sauce and stir, continuing to cook for 2-3 minutes.

Add lentils and enough water to cover them. Reduce heat, cover pot and simmer for about 1 hour. Add water to keep lentils covered, if necessary. Makes 2-3 servings.

"Dig in!" But even these eager eaters were hard pressed to complete their meals. The average customer at the Golden Cuisine has to request a "doggy bag." There is just too much food to eat at one sitting.

Fish Soup

1 cup olive oil
2 onions, sliced thick
2 celery branches, chopped
4 garlic cloves, crushed
6 tomatoes, peeled, chopped
10 lg. potatoes, peeled
12 leeks, trimmed
Juice of 1 lemon
2 lb. eel, skinned, sliced
2 lbs. sea bass

4 sprigs parsley
1 cup white wine
6 cups water
4 or 5 fish heads
2 bay leaves
1 tsp. rosemary
2 tsp. whole thyme
2 cups fish broth
2 lb. cod

Saute onions, celery, garlic and bay leaves in olive oil for about 5 minutes.

Add tomatoes, thyme, fish broth, parsley, wine, water, fish heads and rosemary. Bring to boil, then reduce heat and simmer for about 30 minutes. Add potatoes and leeks and cook for an additional 25 minutes.

Strain the broth. Return clear broth to soup pot. Save the leek and potatoes. Add lemon juice, eel and cod, adding water to cover if necessary. Boil for 25 minutes and remove eel and cod.

Sprinkle sea bass with lemon, roll in flour, wrap in a cheese cloth and boil in the broth for about 30 minutes.

Place sea bass in a deep platter, surround with the other fish. Serve the broth with leeks, potatoes, and mix the fish.

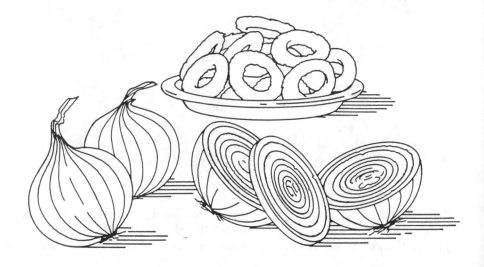

Cassoulet

1 lb. dry white beans	1 lb. salt pork
Water to cover	10 chicken thighs
1 tsp. black pepper	3 Tbsps. oil
6 whole cloves	1 cup chopped onions
2 carrots, sliced	2 cloves minced garlic
1/4 tsp. thyme	1 lb. garlic sausage
1 smoked ham hock	1 cup bread crumbs
3 Tbsps. melted butter	

Soak beans overnight. To cook, place in soup pot and cover with water. Add pepper, cloves, carrots, thyme and ham hock. Bring to boil, cover and simmer for 1-1/2 hours, adding water if necessary.

Cook salt pork in a separate small pan, covering with water and boiling. When done, dice it and add to the beans.

In a skillet, saute chicken thighs in oil until well browned. Remove chicken and add onions and garlic and saute until tender.

Cut the sausage into 1-inch pieces. Add the onion and garlic to the beans, stirring well. Layer the beans, meats and the chicken in a 6 quart casserole. Cover and bake at 350° for 3 hours. Add water as needed to keep covered.

Mix the dry bread crumbs with melted butter. Sprinkle over the beans and then bake uncovered for 30 minutes more. Makes 10 servings.

Nick hosts the Special Olympics.

Minestrone

1 lb. hot Italian sausages	4 cups fresh shelled beans
1 lb. mild Italian sausage	2 quarts water

Pierce sausages. Bring water to boil after adding sausage and beans. Reduce heat and simmer for about 1 hour. Then remove sausages. Puree the beans with 1 cup of the cooking water and return them to the rest of the cooking water.

1/4 lb. Panceta or salt pork	4 Tbsps. olive oil
1/4 cup celery leaves, minced	1 onion, minced
	1/4 cup minced parsley
1 can (1 lb.) pear shaped tomatoes, cubed	1 cup chicken broth
	1 carrot, diced
1/4 cup celery leaves, minced	1 zucchini, thinly sliced
	1 cup coarsely chopped
1 smal potato, peeled, diced	Swiss chard
2 cups coarsely chopped cabbage	

In an 8 quart saucepan, saute the Panceta or salt pork, onion, garlic, celery leaves and parsley in oil until the onions are limp. This should take about 5 minutes.

Add the tomatoes, chicken broth, carrot, diced celery and potato. Cover, bring to a boil and then simmer for 15 minutes.

Add the zucchini, cabbage and Swiss chard. Continue to simmer for about 10 more minutes.

Remove cover and add 3/4 cup fresh basil leaves, pepper to taste and finally the sliced pre-cooked sausage. Cover again and simmer for about 10 minutes, and serve.

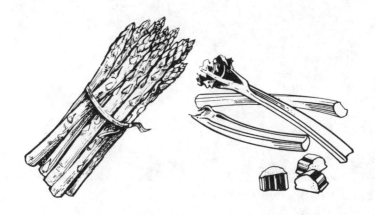

3

Salads

"Nick, it started with pizza, and we've been working our way through the menu. The salads are outstanding, especially the Greek Salad. *"Keep up the good food!"*

Debbie Black

Greek Salad

2 tomatoes, cut into wedges
1 med. cucumber, peeled
  and cubed
1 small red onion, sliced
1 small green pepper, sliced
2 Tbsps. red wine vinegar
Greek oregano

4 green onions, sliced
6 pepperoncinis
1 small onion, sliced
10 Kalamata olives
1/2 lb. Feta cheese
1/4 cup pure olive oil
Whole thyme

Placed wedged tomatoes in a salad platter. Artfully arrange the cucumber, onions and pepper on the platter. Put the olives on top of the salad. Crumble the Feta cheese over the entire platter, and then pour the olive oil over the vegetables.

Sprinkle top with red wine vinegar, and the Greek oregano and thyme.

Makes 2 servings.

Pasta

1 cup white Fusilli pasta
cooked
1/2 cup green Fusilli pasta,
cooked
1/2 cup Gardiniera (mixed
marinated vegetables)
2 Pepperoncinis
2 artichoke hearts
2 cherry peppers
2 slices of zucchini, chopped
6 pitted black olives, sliced
6 pitted green olives, sliced
1/4 cucumber, peeled, cubed
1/8 cup green pepper, sliced
1/8 cup sliced mushrooms
1/8 cup sliced red onions
1/8 cup sliced onion
1/8 cup sliced red pepper
1 Tbsps. chopped red
pimentoes
1/4 tomato, cubed
1 cup Italian dressing

Mix all ingredients in a large bowl. Add 1 cup Italian dressing to the tossed salad before serving. Makes 2-3 servings.

Tortellini Proscuitto

2 lbs. Tortellini
2 green peppers,
thinly sliced
1 red pepper, thinly sliced
1/4 cup chopped red
pimentoes
1 cup pitted black olives,
sliced
1 cup pitted green olives,
sliced
10 oz. Proscuitto, in strips
8 Tbps. olive oil
Juice of 2 lemons
2 Tbsps. Dijon mustard
1 tsp. minced garlic
2 Tbsps. red wine vinegar
1 Tbsps. sweet basil
Pinch of pepper

Cook the Tortellini for 10 minutes, remove from heat and cool. Then place in a bowl with the peppers, pimentoes, olives and strips of Prosciutto.

Mix well the olive oil, lemon juice, mustard, garlic, red wine vinegar, basil and pepper. Add this to the bowl with the pasta, and toss well. Refrigerate.

Makes about 10 servings.

Eggplant Salad

2 tomatoes, peeled,
   chopped
4 shallots, minced
1 Tbsp. chopped fresh
   mint
2 med. eggplants
1 zucchini
2 Tbsps. red wine
   vinegar

10 mint leaves, thickly chopped
Kalamata olives
Pinch of black pepper
1 tsp. grated lemon peel
1 Tbsp. chopped parsley
1 tsp. sweet basil
5 Tbsps. olive oil
1 clove garlic, minced

Slice the eggplants into slabs about one-quarter inch thick. The zucchini should be cut into 1/4" slices.

Combine the tomatoes, shallots, chopped mint, garlic, red wine vinegar, pepper, lemon peel, parsley and sweet basil with 3 Tbsps. of olive oil in a large salad bowl. After combining, arrange on a large serving platter.

Brush the eggplant and zucchini slices with oil amd grill them; then place on the same serving platter. Mix the mint leaves and a pinch of pepper with 2 Tbsps. of olive oil, and sprinkle this over the top of the vegetables. Garnish the salad with Kalamata olives before serving. Makes 4-5 servings.

Shrimp Pasta

1/2 head lettuce, torn
1 cup small cooked shrimp
1 small bell pepper, sliced
4 green onions, sliced
1/2 red onion, sliced
4 mushrooms, sliced
1/2 cup green Fussili
   pasta, cooked

1 small tomato, diced
1/2 small cucumber, diced
1/8 cup sliced black olive
1/8 cup sliced green olive
1/2 cup white Fusilli pasta,
   cooked
Pinch black pepper

Place lettuce on plate. Top lettuce with the shrimp, then cover shrimp with the remainder of the ingredients. Top salad vegetables with the white and green pasta. 2-3 servings.

Golden Salad

1/2 head lettuce	2 tomatoes, diced
2 slices of ham	3 green onions, chopped
1 head Romaine lettuce	2 eggs, hardboiled, diced
1/2 bunch watercress	1/2 cup Roquefort
1 whole chicken breast	cheese, crumbled
1/2 cup sliced black olives	8 strips of bacon

Cook and dice the bacon and chicken breast. Chop the lettuce and watercress coarsely and toss together. Place on a serving platter along with the ham.

Arrange the tomatoes, onions, chicken, olives, bacon, and eggs on platter, and sprinkle the Roquefort cheese on top.

DRESSING:

1/4 cup wine vinegar	1 tsp. dry mustard
1/2 tsp. Worchestershire	1 clove garlic, minced
sauce	1/4 cup water
2 Tbsps. lemon juice	1/8 cup sugar
1/2 tsp. pepper	1/4 cup olive oil
3/4 cup vegetable oil	

Mix all the ingredients well, and serve with salad. Makes 5 to 6 servings.

Nick and Cheryl Parker, Channel 12 News.

Sliced Lamb Salad

2 green peppers
2 red peppers
1/2 cup chopped
   green onions
1 lb. cold lamb,
   cut into strips
2 Tbsps. Worchestershire sauce

2 Tbsps. Dijon mustard
2 Tbsps. red wine vinegar
1/2 cup olive oil
1/2 tsp. pepper
1/8 cup parsley, chopped

Wrap green and red peppers in a foil and cook in 350° oven for about 30 minutes. Then skin and seed the peppers, and cut them into thin strips.

Mix the onions and lamb meat with the peppers. Then separately mix thoroughly the mustard, red wine vinegar, Worchestershire sauce, olive oil, pepper and parsley. Add this to the lamb and pepper mixture and mix well. Makes about 4 servings.

Crab Avocado Salad

1/2 head of lettuce
1/2 cup cooked crab meat
1/2 cup shredded Mozzarella
2 whole artichoke hearts
1/2 green pepper, sliced
1/2 red pepper, sliced
1/2 red onion, sliced

1 small avocado
1/4 cup black olives
1/4 cup green olives
1/2 cucumber, diced
1 sm. tomato, diced
6 mushrooms, sliced

Tear lettuce leaves from head and place on a salad plate. Spread the crab meat over the lettuce. Then artfully place the peppers, onion, mushrooms, artichoke hearts, tomato and cucumber over the crab meat.

Slice the small avocado and place the slices over the mixed vegetables. Lay the shredded Mozzarella cheese over the avocado, and finally top the salad with the olives.

"Enjoy!"

Antipasto

In a large salad bowl, stack from bottom to the top:

1/2 heat of torn lettuce
1/2 small cucumber, cubed
1/2 small onion, sliced
1/2 small red onion, sliced
4 slices cheddar cheese,
   cut into strips
2 slices salami,
   cut into strips
2 slices Mortadella,
   cut into strips
2 slices ham, cut into strips
1/2 cup mixed marinated
   vegetables
1/4 cup cooked Fusilli pasta

1/2 small tomato, cubed
1/2 small green pepper
1/2 small red pepper
4 med. sliced mushrooms
8 pitted black olives
8 green olives
2 pepperoncinis
2 cherry peppers
2 artichoke hearts
1 hardboiled egg, sliced
6 slices pepperoni
Chopped pimentoes
Italian dressing

Top with the pasta, slices of hardboiled egg and the slices of pepperoni. Sprinkle the chopped pimentoes on top.

Serve the Antipasto with Italian dressing. Makes 2 to 3 servings.

The Phoenix Gazette   Fri., March 27, 1987 5N-5

Restaurant owner considers a finished meal a failure

By Dave Eskes
The Phoenix Gazette

SCOTTSDALE — Publisher Brad Steiger spoke of Nick Ligidakis' Golden Pizzeria with a reverence customarily reserved for Michelangelo's statue of "David."

"I was picking up some photos at Image Craft," he began, "when I got the hungries. So I stopped by Nick's

In it, you will find everything from fish roe salad to fried milk. But most recipes are staples such as Eggplant Mousaka, Veal Skordato and Stuffed Eggplant Leaves. And most use common ingredients.

"Nick's Creative Cooking" is a local production, with black and white photos of Ligidakis hard at work, while

4

Pocket Roll Sandwiches and Croissants

Pepper Steak

3 oz. skirt or flank steak
4 Tbsps. frying oil
3 Tbsps. red cooking wine
1 sm. red bell pepper
1 sm. green bell pepper
4 mushrooms, thinly sliced
1 Tbsp. sliced black olives
1 Tbsp. sliced green olives

1 Tbsp. steak sauce
1 tsp. Worchestershire sauce
1 tsp. soy sauce
1/2 tsp. hot chili
1 small onion
10" sub roll or French bread

Saute the steak and oil in a skillet. Add the red cooking wine.

Thinly slice the bell peppers, onion, mushroom and olives. Add to the saucepan of meat and stir. Add the steak sauce, Worchestershire, soy sauce and chili. Saute until the vegetables are soft, about 5-8 minutes.

Make a horizontal slice into the side of the bread, creating a pocket. Spoon fill the pepper steak and vegetables into the pocket.

Place 2 slices of tomato and 4 thin slices of Swiss cheese over the opening of the pocket.

Bake in a 350° oven, for about 10 minutes.

Golden Steak

One 8 oz. skirt steak
1/2 cup vegetable oil
1/8 cup red wine vinegar
1 tsp. Greek oregano
1 tsp. basil
1 tsp. thyme
Pinch of black pepper

4 Tbsps. cooking oil
8-inch long French bread
4 slices Provolone cheese
1 onion, sliced thinly
1 green pepper, sliced
thinly

Marinate the steak in the vegetable oil, red wine vinegar, oregano, basil, thyme and pepper mixture for 2-3 hours.

Saute the steak in the cooking oil for about 4 minutes on each side. Saute the green pepper and onion until soft.

Slice the French bread lengthwise. Place steak on the bottom half of the bread. Top steak with the peppers and onions. Place the Provolone cheese atop the steak and bake in a 350° oven, until the cheese is melted.

Tuna Melt

4 oz. white tuna
4 Tbsps. mayonnaise
1 Tbsp. chopped onion
Pinch of black pepper
1 Tbsp. chopped green olives
2 Tbsps. dill pickle relish

10" Italian or
French bread
2 slices of tomato
4 slices of Swiss cheese
1 Tbsp. Dijon mustard

Mix the tuna, mayonnaise, mustard, onions, pepper, relish and green olives well. Slice the bread lengthwise on the side to make a pocket.

Spoon tuna filling into the pocket. Place the tomato slices on top of the tuna salad at top of the pocket. Place the Swiss cheese on top of the tomatoes, covering the opening of the pocket in the bread.

Bake in a 350° oven until the cheese is melted.

Reuben Sandwich

6 oz. sliced Pastrami
3 oz. sauerkraut
2 Tbsps. Thousand Island
  dressing
2 Tbsps. cooking oil

4 slices Swiss cheese
10" French or
  Italian bread

Grill the pastrami and sauerkraut in the cooking oil until the pastrami is soft. Mix the Thousand Island dressing with the pastrami and sauerkraut.

Make a pocket lengthwise in the side of the bread and spoon the filling inside. Top the opening of the break pocket with the Swiss cheese. Bake in a 350° oven, until the cheese is melted.

Feta Sub

6 oz. Gyros meat
2 Tbsps. Feta dressing
1 Tbsp. sliced black olives
1 cup red onion, sliced thin

10" Italian bread
3 oz. Feta cheese
1 oz. Riccota cheese
2 Tbsps. butter

Saute meat and onion in butter until onions are soft. Place the meat and onions in a bowl and add the Feta dressing and olives.

Slice the bread on the side lengthwise to make a pocket. Spoon the stuffing inside. Mix the Feta and Riccota cheese and place on top of the pocket. Bake in 350° oven until cheese is lightly browned.

Monte Cristo

6 oz. cooked turkey,
  sliced thinly
4 oz. cooked ham,
  sliced thinly
10" French or Italian bread

2 Tbsps. butter
1 egg, beaten
1 Tbsp. milk
4 slices Swiss cheese

Mix the turkey, ham, egg and milk well. Melt butter in a skillet and add the mixture, frying until lightly browned. Slice the bread on the side lengthwise to make a pocket. Spoon the mixture into the pocket. Top the opening with the slices of Swiss cheese.

Bake in a 350° oven until the cheese is melted.

Baked Egg

1 tsp. grated
  Parmesan cheese
2 oz. shredded
  Mozzarella
2 oz. shredded Provolone
10" Italian or
  French bread

3 mushrooms, sliced
2 eggs
1 Tbsp. butter
2 Tbsps. Riccota
  cheese

Saute mushrooms in butter until soft. Mix the 4 cheeses with the eggs and add to the skillet. Fry, stirring well.

Slice the bread lengthwise to make a pocket. Spoon the filling inside. Bake in 350° oven for 6-8 minutes, or until the top of the filling is brown.

"Each dish, individually prepared, is a unique taste experience.
"Very enjoyable.
"Very original."

Stacey Leigh

"Simply delicious. From sight to taste, all is exquisite."

Paul Leigh

Meatball

10" Italian bread
3 oz. shredded
  Mozzarella

1 meatball
6 Tbsps. meat sauce

Slice the bread lengthwise on the side to make a pocket. Put the meatball in the pocket, cover with meat sauce. Fill the pocket opening with the shredded cheese and bake in an oven at 350° until the cheese is melted.

Sausage Sandwich

1 mild Italian sausage,
  sliced
3 oz. shredded
  Mozzarella

6 Tbsps. meat sauce
10" Italian bread

Slice bread on the side lengthwise to make a pocket. Place slices of sausage in the pocket and spoon the meat sauce in on top. Fill the bread opening with the Mozzarella cheese. Bake in a 350° oven until the cheese is melted.

B-B-Q Beef Sandwich

8 oz. sliced roast beef
1/4 cup B-B-Q sauce
4 slices of cheddar cheese

2 Tbsps. butter
1 small onion, chopped
10" Italian bread

Saute roast beef and onion in butter until soft. Place B-B-Q sauce in a bowl and mix with the beef and onions. Slice the bread on the side lengthwise to make a pocket. Spoon stuffing into the pocket and place the sliced cheddar cheese over the opening in the bread. Bake in 350° oven until cheese is melted.

Bleu Roast Sandwich

8 oz. sliced roast beef
2 Tbsps. bleu cheese,
  crumbled
4 slices Swiss cheese

1 Tbsp. bleu cheese dressing
2 Tbsps. butter
1 med. red onion
10" Italian bread

Saute roast beef and onion in butter until soft. Place dressing and crumbled bleu cheese in a bowl and add the sauteed meat. Mix well. Slit the bread horizontally on the side to make a pocket. Spoon the stuffing into the pocket and top the opening with the slices of cheese. Bake in a 350° oven until the cheese is melted.

Burgers

1/2 lb. 100% ground beef

Shape into a long patty, about 10-inches long. Grill to your preference (rare, medium, well), and serve on Italian bread with your choice of freshly sliced condiments.

Burger Variations

Bacon Burger

Top basic burger with 3 slices of cheddar cheese and 3 slices of cooked bacon.

Western Burger

3 slices of Canadian bacon   3 slices of ham
3 slices of cheddar cheese   2 Tbsps. B-B-Q sauce

Top basic burger with meat and cheese. After the cheese has melted, top the burger with B-B-Q sauce before placing on bread or bun.

Californian

3 slices cheddar cheese   1/2 avocado, sliced
3 slices of cooked ham

Hawaiian

3 slices of Canadian bacon   1 Tbsp. pineapple tidbits
3 slices of Swiss cheese

Top basic burger with bacon, cheese and pineapple. Just before serving on Italian bread or a bun, top the meat with a tablespoon of Thousand Island dressing.

Italian Burger

Top burger with 2 Tbsps. pizza sauce, 3 slices of Canadian bacon and 4 slices of Mozzarella cheese.

Athenian Burger

1/2 lb. 100% ground beef   3 oz. Feta cheese
1 Tbsp. sliced black olives   1 Tbsp. yogurt sauce
4 green pepperoncinis

Shape meat into a patty about 10-inches long, as for the basic burger on page 38. Top with the Feta cheese and black olives while grilling. Just before serving with regular sandwich condiments, top with the yogurt sauce and the Greek pepperoncinis.

Croissants

Oscar Beef

1/4 lb. ground beef   1 Tbsp. butter
4 asparagus spears   2 oz. crabmeat

Grill the ground beef to your personal liking. Saute the asparagus and crabmeat in butter until soft.
Place the hamburger on the bottom part of a croissant roll. Spoon the crabmeat mixture on top.

"Nick Ligidakis' Golden Cuisine is extraordinary! Stupendous! I have eaten all over the world and have never had more authentic European cuisine, prepared with natural ingredients by a Master Chef who CARES!!!"

**Eileen Goldberg
Highland Park, IL**

"The Flakey Gold Club Croissant Sandwich filled with delicate turkey, bacon and cheese is by far the best sandwich I've eaten."

Justin Menendez

Francheese Croissant

2 slices of cheddar cheese   1 jumbo hot dog
3 slices of bacon

Slice the hot dog lengthwise to make a pocket. Place the cheddar cheese in the pocket, and wrap the bacon around the cheese filled hot dog. Secure with toothpicks.

Bake in 350° oven until bacon is crispy. Place in croissant and serve with Dijon mustard.

Avocado Crab Croissant

4 slices of Swiss cheese   3 oz. crabmeat
1 croissant roll   1/2 avocado, sliced

Place crabmeat on bottom part of croissant. Put slices of avocado on top of the crabmeat, then the slices of Swiss cheese. Bake in 350° oven until cheese is melted.

Shrimp Pineapple Croissant

2 Tbsps. pineapple bits   2 Tbsps. butter
3 oz. baby shrimp   4 green onions, chopped
4 slices of Swiss cheese   1 Tbsp. white wine

Saute shrimp and onion in butter until the onions are soft. Add the white wine, then the pineapple bits and saute for 2 minutes longer. Place this mixture on the bottom slice of the croissant. Top with the Swiss cheese. Bake in a 350° oven until the cheese is melted.

5

Calzone

Vegetable Calzone

Place a 12" Pizza Round on a working surface.

1 whole artichoke heart,
   sliced
1 Tbsp. chopped zucchini
1 Tbsp. sliced black olive
1 Tbsp. sliced green olives
1 Tbsp. green peppers
1/2 small onion, chopped
4 mushrooms, sliced

1 Tbsp. Riccota cheese
1 tsp. Romano, grated
1 tsp. Parmesan, grated
2 oz. shredded Mozzarella
1 oz. shredded Provolone
1/2 red onion, chopped
4 Tbsps. pizza sauce

Mix ingredients well. Place the mixture on the middle of the round. Fold dough like a turnover. With a fork, press the ends to seal the Calzone. Pierce a few holes on the top of the dough. Bake in 425° oven for about 20 minutes, until brown on top.

Cheese Calzone

2 oz. Riccota cheese
2 oz. shredded Mozzarella
2 oz. shredded Provolone
2 oz. shredded Monterey
   Jack

1 oz. Feta cheese
1/2 oz. grated Romano
1/2 oz. grated Parmesan
1 egg

Mix ingredients well. Follow the same directions as for the Vegetable Calzone (above).

"My favorite dish is the Cheese Calzone. The cheeses that Nick uses are superb, very good quality, blended very well together. Then, there's the dough; absolutely great! Such fluffiness! Very good stuff."

Lesley Potter

Meat Ball or Sausage Calzone

5 Tbsps. meat sauce
1 meat ball or
  1 sausage, sliced
2 oz. shredded Mozzarella
2 oz. shredded Provolone

1 Tbsp. Riccota cheese
1 tsp. grated Parmesan
1 tsp. grated Romano
2 mushrooms, sliced

Mix all ingredients well. Prepare by following the directions for making the Vegetable Calzone, on page ??.

Nick — "Cooking with Rita Davenport."

6

Pizza

"The pizza at **Golden Cuisine** *is the standard by which all other pizzas are judged. I've never had better anywhere."*

Frank Heffner

Pizza Dough

4 cups lukewarm water
3/4 oz. vegetable oil
4 lbs. of unbleached flour
1/4 cup sugar
1/8 lb. margarine melted

3/4 oz. yeast
1 medium egg
1 cup milk
1/8 cup salt

Put lukewarm water in a large mixing bowl. Set mixer at low speed. Add the yeast to the bowl and mix for about 5 minutes.

Add the egg, milk, vegetable oil, salt, sugar and melted butter to the bowl. Mix on low speed for another 5 minutes.

Add the flour and let mix for about 8 to 10 minutes, until the dough is elastic and soft. If dough is still sticky, add a little flour.

Place dough on a working surface. Cut off 1 lb. pieces of dough and form into balls. Place the balls on a metal sheet, a few inches apart. Cover them with plastic bags. Refrigerate overnight. The next day, the balls should be raised to about double in size.

To make Rounds:

Place ball in the palms of your hand and with the tips of your fingers work the ball, so you will make a round disk. This may require a little practice.

Place dough disk on a floured surface. Knead with your fingertips on both sides of the round, then press the round with the palm of your hand to flatten. Be certain the dough is always round. With a rolling pin, roll the dough out to about 12" in diameter. Place dough in a round carton, sprinkle with flour, cover, and let it rise for about 2 hours.

To Assemble Pizza:

Place round on a greased pizza pan. Spoon about 5 tablespoons of pizza sauce on the middle, and spread it evenly on top of the round, up to 2-inches away from the edge. Top the sauce with shredded Mozzarella cheese. Place other desired toppings over the cheese.

Cover the toppings with a mixture of shredded Provolone and shredded white cheddar cheese.

Place in a preheated 425° oven and bake for about 20 minutes, or until the edges of the crust are golden brown and the cheese is lightly browned.

> *"My friends say they'd fly in from Tulsa, OK for one of Nick's pizzas. They are absolutely the best!"*
>
> **Karla & Ronnie Jones**

> *"I love to eat at Nick's Golden Cuisine. No matter what I order, it is always so tasty and I have some left over to take home to enjoy the following day as the portions are so large."*
>
> **Martha Bennett**

Whole Wheat Crust

1-1/2 cups warm water	1/2 tsp. salt
1 pack of dry yeast	1 tsp. sweet basil
2 Tbsps. salad oil	1 tsp. Greek oregano
1-1/2 cups unbleached flour	1/4 cup whole wheat germ
1-1/2 cups whole wheat flour	1 tsp. sugar
2 Tbsps. melted margarine	2 Tbsps. milk

Dissolve yeast in warm water and mix thoroughly. Add salt, salad oil, sugar, sweet basil, Greek oregano, whole wheat germ, melted margarine and milk to the yeast and mix well.

Add the unbleached and whole wheat flour. Mix well.

Knead on a floured surface until dough is smooth and elastic. Place in a greased bowl and cover. Let rise until double, for about 45 minutes.

Makes two 14" pizza rounds.

Egg Pasta

Most of the cooks make their own pasta. Once you have tried, you will probably never want dry pasta again. Try it. It's easier than you think.

4 cups unbleached flour	6 eggs
1/2 tsp. salt	5 tsps. salad oil

Place flour in a large bowl. Add egg, oil and salt. Mix until you make a soft dough ball.

Place on a lightly floured working surface. Knead until elastic and smooth. Cover with a dampened cloth; let stand about half an hour.

Divide into quarters. Roll out on a lightly floured board with a rolling pin, to about 1/8" thickness. Cut to desired size. Makes 2 lbs. pasta.

Green Pasta

3-1/2 cups unbleached flour	3 medium eggs
10 oz. fresh or cooked, drained and minced spinach	3 tsp. salad oil 1/2 tsp. salt

Mix and follow the same proportions as for the Egg Pasta (above). This dough takes a little longer to set during the kneading and rolling process, because of the spinach in it.

Cooking time of the Pasta varies. It ranges fro 4 to 6 minutes. The water should be boiling. Pasta should be cooked *el dente*, and is done when it has a little resistance to a bite.

Linguini or Spaghetti — cut into strips 1/8" wide.

Fettucini — cut into 1/4" strips.

Lasagne — cut into 4" wide strips.

Maniccotti — cut into 4" x 6" strips.

Ravioli — squares.

Tortellini — small twists.

Agnolotti — round Ravioli.

Cappaletti — little hats.

Fillings for stuffed pasta are many. You probably can create your own, according to your taste.

Here are some:

Cappaletti

1/4 lb. ground pork	1 tsp. lemond rind
1/4 lb. ground beef	1/2 tsp. nutmeg
1/4 lb. ground chicken	1/8 cup grated Parmesan
1/8 lb. ground salt pork	1 Tbsp. grated Romano
1 garlic clove	1/2 tsp. black pepper
1 egg	

Saute meats, garlic, lemon rind and nutmeg until brown. Add the grated cheese, pepper and egg. Stir for a few second and remove from the heat.

Use 2 lbs. of pasta, rolled into 1/8" thickness. Cut pieces into circles about 2-inches in diameter. Place a little filling in the center. Fold to half circles. Seal the ends. Wrap the pasta around the index finger, overlapping opposite ends. Press them together and seal tight.

Bend the upper edge of the arch outward a little at a time to form brim.

Place in a tray dusted with flour. Makes about 100.

Agnolotti

1-1/2 cups spinach	1 cup Riccota
3 oz. shredded cheddar	3 oz. grated Romano
1 oz. grated Parmesan	Pinch of nutmeg
1 garlic clove, minced	Pinch of pepper
Use 2 lbs. pasta	

Rinse spinach and cut the stems. Cook until wilted. Dry the leaves and place them in a bowl.

Add the cheeses, nutmeg, pepper and garlic to the spinach and mix well.

Divide the pasta into two pieces. Roll out to 1/8" thickness. Cut into strips 4" wide. Place 1 tablespoon of filling on one of the strips, about 2-inches apart. Cut with a round cutter. Fold to form half-moon shape. Moisten ends. Press with fork to seal. Place in a tray, floured. Makes 8 to 10 servings.

Ravioli

1/4 lb. shredded Mozzarella
1/8 cup grated Parmesan
1/8 cup grated Romano
2 tsp. chopped parsley
2 cups Riccota
2 eggs, beaten
1 Tbsp. chopped chives
1/2 tsp. pepper

Divide 2 lbs. of pasta dough into 2 parts. Roll to 1/8" thickness. Place 1 teaspoon of the filling about 1-1/2" apart. Cover with the second sheet of rolled dough. Cut into squares. Moisten edges, and seal with a fork. Place in a tray and dust with flour. Makes about 8 servings.

Tortellini

1/2 lb. skinless chicken
  breasts, coooked and
  ground
1 Tbsp. grated Parmesan
2 egg yolks
1/2 lb. ham, ground
2 Tbsps. grated Romano
1/2 tsp. pepper
1/2 tsp. nutmeg

Mix meat, cheese, egg yolks and seasonings well together. Divide 2 lbs. of pasta dough into 4 parts. Roll out to 1/8" thickness and cut into circles about 1-1/2" in diameter. Place 1/2 teaspoon of filling in the center of each circle. Fold to form a half-moon shape, moisten the edges and seal. Bring the two edges together to form a ring, and seal.

Place in a tray, dust with flour. Makes 8-10 servings.

Other Fillings

4 oz. veal, ground and fried
1 tsp. nutmeg
1/8 grated Parmesan
6 oz. spinach
1 egg
1/2 tsp. pepper

Mix well together and use as pasta filling.

Other Fillings (Continued)

4 oz. chicken breast,
  cut into pieces
2 oz. Mortadella, chopped
3 oz. veal, cut into pieces
3 oz. ground pork
2 Tbsps. butter

1 Tbsp. chopped parsley
1 Tbsp. Parmesan cheese
2 Tbsps. grated Romano
1 tsp. nutmeg
1 egg

Saute meat in butter until brown. Grind the parsley, egg, cheeses and nutmeg, and mix well with the sauteed meats. Stir thoroughly.

3 lbs. spinach, cooked
  and ground
1/4 cup Parmesan cheese
1/4 cup Romano, grated

1-1/2 cups Riccota
3 egg yolks
1/2 tsp. pepper

Mix ingredients well. Use as pasta filling.

1-1/2 lbs. spinach,
  cooked and ground
2 oz. grated Parmesan
1 oz. grated Romano

4 oz. Prosciutto, ground
1 cup Riccota
1 tsp. pepper
1/2 tsp. nutmeg

Mix ingredients thoroughly.

2 Tbsps. butter
2 Tbsps. chopped onions
1 garlic clove, minced
3/4 lb. mushrooms, sliced

8 oz. cream cheese
1 tsp. basil, chopped
1 tsp. thyme, chopped
1/2 tsp. pepper

Saute onions, garlic and mushrooms in butter until onions are soft. Remove from heat. When cool, mix vegetables with cream cheese and spices and puree in a blender to make the pasta filling.

Spaghetti Carbonara

2 oz. ham, coarsely
  chopped
1 Tbsp. green pepper,
  coarsely chopped
1 Tbsp. red pepper,
  coarsely chopped
2 strips of bacon, in pieces

2 Tbsps. butter
2 cloves of garlic, chopped
Pepper, to taste
1/2 pint whipping cream
1/4 lb. cooked spaghetti
1/2 cup grated Romano

Using the butter in a heavy skillet, saute the meat and peppers for 6-8 minutes. Add the garlic and pepper and saute for 3-4 minutes more. Then add the whipping cream to the skillet, over a very low heat. Add the cooked spaghetti to the skillet, stirring well. Stir in the cheese and cook for a final 3-5 minutes. Makes 1 serving.

"I go to the Golden Cuisine *every week because the food and service are superb. Nick uses only the finest ingredients in his cooking while his wife, Karen, makes every customer feel special with her warm smile. My favorites are the* Spaghetti Carbonara *and the pizza."*

Toby Weissert

"I have known Nick for over a year now, eating at his place several times a week, and I have yet to make it completely through the menu. My favorite dishes so far are the Tortellini Romanolla *(next page), the Dolmades, the Gyro, and the leg of lamb. All are exceptional not only for the quality of ingredients chosen, but more importantly for his unique blending of ingredients and spices to create, rich, distinctive dishes."*

William F. Welsh

Tortellini Romanolla

1 Tbsp. coarsely chopped
  walnuts
1/2 pint whipping cream
1/4 lb. meat stuffed
  Tortellini, cooked

1 Tbsp. butter
Pinch of black pepper
1/2 cup grated Romano
1/2 cup grated Parmesan

Place walnuts and butter in a heavy skillet over a low heat for 1-2 minutes. Add the whipping cream and pepper and continue to cook for another 2-3 minutes. Add the Tortellini to the skillet and cook for about 3 minutes. Finally add the cheese and cook, stirring, for 3-4 minutes. Makes 1 serving.

Fettuccine Formaggi

1/4 lb. fresh cooked
  Fettuccine noodles
1/4 cup shredded
  Mozzarella
1/4 cup Riccota cheese
1/8 cup shredded
  Provolone cheese

1/4 cup grated Parmesan
1/2 pint whipping cream
Pinch of black pepper
2 Tbsps. butter
4 mushrooms, sliced
1/8 cup grated Romano
  cheese

Melt butter in a heavy skillet. Add the mushrooms and saute until light brown. Add the whipping cream and pepper and turn the heat to low.

Stir the Riccota, Mozzarella and Provolone cheeses into the skillet, for about 3 to 4 minutes or until the cheese is completely melted. Add the Fettuccini and stir thoroughly. Finally add the grated Romano and Parmesan, stirring and cooking until thick, for about another 3 to 4 minutes. Makes 1 serving.

"The Fettuccini Formaggi *is a pasta and cheese lover's heaven! Nick's special touches put me on Cloud Nine!"*

Kristie

"I've never been able to pronounce all the items on Nick's menu, but I always enjoy them.
"Nick's pizza is fantastic, but his wife's cookies can't be beat.
"I'm a 'Nick Lasagne Addict' — now receiving counseling."

Wally Olsen

Lasagne Il Re

5 oz. cooked Lasagne
  noodles
1 tsp. ground cinnamon
Black pepper, to taste
4 oz. shredded Mozzarella
1 tsp. grated Romano cheese
1 tsp. grated Parmesan cheese

4 oz. meat sauce
1 oz. Riccota cheese
2 mushrooms, sliced
1/2 tsp. parsley
3 oz. additional meat
  sauce

Place cooked Lasagne noodles in a small casserole. Add the 4 oz. of meat sauce and toss noodles to mix well. Break the Riccota cheese into small pieces and place in the casserole.

Add the sliced mushrooms and sprinkle the cinnamon, pepper, parsley, and grated Romano and Parmesan on top. Place the additional 3 oz. of meat sauce in the casserole and sprinkle the shredded Mozzarella on top of the sauce. Place in a 375° oven and bake for about 30 minutes, or until the cheese is golden brown. Makes 1 serving.

Ravioli Bolognese

1 mild Italian sausage,
  sliced
1 Tbsp. grated Romano cheese
1 Tbsp. grated Parmesan

6 oz. cooked Ravioli
1 cup meat sauce
1 more cup meat
  sauce

Place the cooked Ravioli in a baking dish. Add a cup of meat sauce and toss with the Ravioli. Mix in the sliced Italian sausage, then sprinkle the grated cheeses on top. Pour the final cup of meat sauce over the sausage and Ravioli.

Bake at 375° for about 20 minutes. Makes 1 serving.

Stuffed Shells Spinaci

5 jumbo pasta shells, parboiled

1-1/2 oz. shredded Mozzarella

1 oz. shredded Provolone cheese

1/2 oz. Feta cheese, crumbled

4 oz. cooked spinach, chopped

4 oz. can of whole tomatoes, in juice

1 egg

1 Tbsp. grated Romano

1 Tbsp. grated Parmesan

4 oz. Riccota cheese

1/2 cup butter

1/2 onion, thinly sliced

2 cloves garlic

Place the pasta shells in a small cooking casserole. In a separate bowl, mix the egg, cheeses and spinach well. Put this mixture in the casserole on top of the pasta shells.

Melt the butter in a skillet. Add the onion and saute until soft, then add the garlic and saute for another 2 minutes. Break the tomatoes and add them to the skillet along with the juice. Then add the following spices and stir well:

Black pepper to taste

1 tsp. sweet basil

1 tsp. Romano cheese

1 tsp. whole thyme

1 tsp. Greek oregano

1 tsp. parsley

Cook the skillet contents for 5 to 6 minutes. Then pour the sauce over the spinach filling and pasta. Bake in a 375° oven for about 25 to 30 minutes. Makes 1 serving.

"Each dish is like an original work of art beautifully presented, pleasing to the eye and the palate — made to enjoy!"

Kay Petros

" 'The Place' where you bring your friends and enjoy your wonderful food."

Lou Petros

Mostaccioli Primo

1/2 onion, thinly sliced
2 whole artichoke hearts,
  (not marinated)
2 Tbsps. white cooking wine
6 oz. cooked Mostaccioli
  noodles, cooked *el dente*
5 oz. shredded Mozzarella cheese

1/4 cup butter
1 cup whipping cream
Black pepper, to taste
1 oz. Riccota cheese
1 oz. grated Romano
1 oz. grated
  Parmesan

Melt butter in a heavy skillet. Break the artichoke hearts into pieces and add them and the onion to the skillet. Saute until onions are soft and then add the cooking wine. Stir in the whipping cream and black pepper. Add the Riccota cheese and stir until the cheese is melted. Add the Mostaccioli noodles to the skillet, then the Romano and Parmesan. Stir well over low heat for 3 to 4 minutes.

Pour the mixture from the skillet into a small baking dish. Top with the shredded Mozzarella and bake in a 375° oven for about 25 minutes, or until the cheese is golden brown. Makes 1 serving.

Clam Linguini

1/4 cup chopped clams
2 cloves garlic, chopped
1 tsp. Greek oregano
1/4 tsp. hot red chili
  peppers
1 tsp. parsley
1/4 cup white cooking
  wine
1/4 lb. cooked Linguini noodles

1/4 cup butter
1 tsp. whole thyme
1 tsp. sweet basil
1/2 tsp. whole
  rosemary
1 oz. grated Romano
1 oz. grated
  Parmesan

Melt butter in a skillet. Saute the clams until soft. Add the garlic and saute for another 3-4 minutes. While stirring, add the thyme, oregano, basil, rosemary, chili peppers, parsley and grated cheeses to the skillet. Pour the cooking wine over the mixture while cooking over low heat for about 5 minutes.

Use the sauce to top the cooked Linguini noodles. Makes 1 serving.

For Red Clam Sauce: add 2 ounces of whole tomatoes in juice after you pour the wine.

"I found Nick's Manicotti Sauce to be delicately balanced; sweet as ripe tomatoes should be; rich with the fresh flavors of the garden. Blessed with such a sauce, the al dente pasta wrapped around a superb blend of cheeses could only be a perfect entree."

Lyle Urick

Maniccotti Marinara

2 pieces of fresh pasta strips about 10" long and 5" wide. (You can use Lasagne noodles, cooked *al dente* if fresh pasta is not available.) Lay the pasta strips on a working surface.

1-1/2 oz. shredded Mozzarella 1 egg, beaten
1-1/2 oz. shredded Provolone 3/4 cup Riccota cheese
1/2 oz. Feta cheese 1 Tbsp. grated Romano
4 oz. can of whole tomatoes 1 Tbsp. grated Parmesan
  in juice, broken 2 Tbsps. butter
2 cloves of chopped garlic 1/2 onion, thinly sliced
Pinch of black pepper 1 tsp. thyme
1 tsp. basil 1 tsp. oregano
1 tsp. grated Romano 1 tsp. parsley

Beat egg in a bowl. Add Riccota, Mozzarella, Provolone, Feta, Romano and Parmesan cheese. Mix well. Divide mixture into two parts. Place each half on the end of each strip of pasta. Roll into two pasta tubes.

Place the Maniccotti in a baking dish.

Melt the butter in a skillet. Saute the onions and garlic until the onions are soft. Add the broken tomatoes and juice to the skillet. Then stir in the black pepper, thyme, oregano, basil, parsley and grated Romano cheese. Cook for about 5 minutes. Pour sauce over the Maniccotti and bake in a 375° oven for about 25 minutes. Makes 1 serving.

Fusilli Privavera

1 broccoli flowerette, chopped
1/2 cup zucchini, chopped
1 whole artichoke heart, chopped
1/8 cup sliced black olive
1/8 cup sliced green olive
2 cloves garlic, chopped
1 cup white Fusilli pasta, cooked
1 cup green Fusilli pasta, cooked
1 Tbsp. chopped pimentoes
1/4 cup vegetable oil
1/2 small onion
1/2 small red onion
1/2 red pepper
1/2 green pepper
4 mushrooms
1/2 pint whipping cream
Black pepper, to taste
1/2 cup grated Romano
1/2 cup grated Parmesan

Heat oil in a heavy saucepan. Slice all the vegetables thin. Saute onions, peppers and mushrooms for 3-4 minutes; stir in the chopped broccoli and zucchini, saute for another 2-3 minutes.

Add the garlic, olives and artichoke hearts and continue to saute for 3-4 minutes. Then pour in the whipping cream and black pepper, cooking on low heat for about 4 minutes. Add the Fusilli pasta and stir well. Then add the pimentoes and finish with the grated Romano and Parmesan. Stir well and cook for another 2-3 minutes. Makes 1-2 servings.

Linguini Pesce

1/4 lb. cooked Linguini noodles
4 oz. small bay shrimp
1/8 cup white cooking wine
1 Tbsp. grated Romano cheese
1/4 pint whipping cream
1 tsp. parsley
1 tsp. rosemary
1/4 cup olive oil
3 asparagus spears, cut into small pieces
6 mushrooms, sliced
3 oz. crabmeat
1 clove garlic
Pepper, to taste

Heat olive oil in a heavy skillet. Add asparagus pieces and saute for 2 minutes, then add the mushrooms, crabmeat and shrimp and saute for another 3-4 minutes. After adding the garlic, saute for 2 more minutes. Turn heat to low and pour in the cooking wine and cook for 3 minutes. Add the parsley, rosemary and pepper and cook for 2-3 minutes longer. Finish with the Romano and whipping cream, stir for a few minutes longer. Spoon sauce over Linguini noodles. Makes 1 serving.

Agnolotti Romana

1/4 lb. Agnolotti, cooked
2 oz. Prosciutto, chopped
1 clove garlic, chopped
1/8 cup white cooking wine
3 oz. whole tomatoes in
   juice, crushed

1/4 cup olive oil
1/2 onion, thinly sliced
2 Tbsps. pine nuts
1/2 tsp. nutmeg
Black pepper, to taste
1/4 pint whipping cream

Heat olive oil in a heavy saucepan. Saute the onion, garlic and Prosciutto until onions are soft. Add the wine and the crushed tomatoes and saute for another 3-4 minutes.

Add the pine nuts, nutmeg and pepper to the saucepan and simmer over low heat for 6-7 minutes. Simmer another 2-3 minutes after adding the whipping cream.

Place the cooked Agnolotti in a small baking dish. Pour in half of the sauce. Toss well. Top with the rest of the sauce.

Bake in a 350° oven for about 15 minutes. Makes 1 serving.

Capellini Tonato

1/4 lb. Capellini (Angel
   Hair pasta), cooked
1 Tbsp. sliced black olives
1 clove garlic, chopped
1/8 cup white cooking wine
1 tsp. parsley
1 Tbsp. capers

1/4 cup olive oil
1 small red onion
4 oz. fresh tuna
2 small tomatoes, peeled
1 tsp. sweet basil
1 tsp. rosemary

Heat olive oil in a heavy skillet. Cook the onion until soft. Cut the tuna and tomatoes into small pieces and add. Saute for 5 to 6 minutes as you stir in the olives and garlic. Then add the wine and simmer over low heat for 2-3 minutes. Add the basil, rosemary and parsley and simmer for another 3 minutes. Then add the capers, take the skillet off the heat and stir well. Pour the sauce over the Capellini. Makes 1 serving.

Lemony Chicken

1 whole chicken, cut
  into pieces
1/2 lemon
2 Tbsps. grated lemon
  peel
1/4 cup grated Parmesan
  cheese

1/8 cup grated sharp
  Romano
1/4 cup oil
1/8 cup butter
1/2 cup whipping cream
1 cup green grapes

Coat chicken with flour. Heat oil and butter in a skillet and saute chicken until brown on all sides. Reduce heat and cook for about 15 minutes longer.

Squeeze the juice from the 1/2 lemon into the skillet and add the grated lemon peel. Cook over low heat for 2-3 minutes more. Remove the chicken and place on a serving platter.

Put the grapes in the skillet and cook for 2-3 minutes. Add the grated cheeses and stir well, cooking for 1-2 minutes. Spoon the sauce over the chicken. Makes 2-3 servings.

Chicken Palm

8 oz. breast of chicken
2 whole artichoke hearts,
  crushed
2 hearts of palm, cut
  into small pieces
1/4 cup white cooking wine
2 oz. Swiss cheese, shredded

1/2 cup butter
1 egg, beaten
Black pepper, to taste
1/4 pint whipping cream
1 Tbsp. Dijon mustard
2 oz. pecans, chopped

Heat butter in a heavy skillet. Dip chicken in flour, coat with the beaten egg, and dip back into flour. Put in the skillet and brown well on all sides. Add the artichoke hearts and the hearts of palm, cut into small pieces, and saute for 2-3 minutes. Add the wine and pepper and saute for another 5-6 minutes. Remove the chicken breast and place it on a serving plate.

Add the whipping cream, Swiss cheese and pecans to the skillet. Stir well until the cheese melts. Add the Dijon mustard and stir well. Spoon the sauce over the chicken and serve. Makes 1 serving.

Chicken Bleu

One 8 oz. boneless
  chicken breast
1/2 onion, thinly sliced
2 oz. ham, thinly sliced
1/8 cup whipping cream

1/4 cup bleu cheese,
  crumbled
1/4 cup butter
1 egg, beaten
1/4 cup white wine
Black pepper, to taste

Coat chicken with flour, dip into beaten egg, and dip back into the flour. Melt butter in a heavy skillet and brown the chicken well on all sides. Add the onion and ham and saute until the onions are soft. Add the wine and pepper and stir well. Add the whipping cream and simmer for about 2 more minutes. Remove the chicken and place it on a serving plate.

Add the crumbled bleu cheese to the skillet and stir until melted. Spoon the sauce over the chicken. Makes 1 serving.

Chicken Plaka

8 oz. boneless
  chicken breast
6 oz. sliced fresh
  mushrooms
2 cloves of garlic,
  chopped
2 large artichoke hearts,
  broken up (not
  marinated)

1/8 cup white cooking wine
1/4 pint whipping cream
Flour
1 egg, beaten
1/2 cup butter
1/2 lemon
1 small onion, sliced
Black pepper, to taste
Fettuccini noodles

Coat chicken in flour, then with beaten egg and dip back into flour again. Heat butter in skillet and saute chicken for about 3-4 minutes on all sides to brown evenly. Squeeze juice from the lemon into the skillet. Add the mushrooms, onion, garlic and artichoke hearts and saute for about 4 minutes. Then add the white wine and pepper, reduce heat, and simmer for about 3 minutes. Squeeze in the rest of the juice from the 1/2 lemon. Stir in the whipping cream and stir well for a few minutes. Serve the sauce and chicken over Fettuccini noodles. Makes 1 serving.

"We love the Fettuccini Formaggi — *it's so creamy and rich! And Chris' favorite is the* Chicken Kapama — *the unique blend of cloves and cinnamon with the chicken make it really a special dish. Also the pizza is the best ever!"*

Barbara and Chris Cagley

Chicken Kapama

1-8 oz. boneless breast
  of chicken
1 stick of butter
1/4 cup white wine
8 oz. can of whole
  tomatoes in juice
2 sticks of cinnamon
1/2 tsp. nutmeg
1 serving Fettuccini noodles

Flour
1 egg, beaten
1 small onion, chopped
1 clove garlic, chopped
2 bay leaves
5 cloves
1/2 tsp. cinnamon
Black pepper, to taste

Coat chicken with flour, dip in the beaten egg and coat one more time with flour. Melt butter in a heavy skillet and brown chicken on both sides, about 4-5 minutes to a side. Add the wine to the skillet, then the onion and garlic. Saute until the onion is soft, but not brown.

Crush the tomatoes and add to the skillet with the juice. Turn heat low to simmer and add bay leaves, cinnamon sticks and cinnamon, nutmeg, cloves and pepper. Stir well. Cover and simmer for about 15 minutes.

Serve over an order of Fettuccini noodles. Makes 1 serving.

"Nick Ligidakis, a great cook and an excellent father. He's got a great restaurant. If you come to his Golden Cuisine *I recommend* Chicken Picata. *That's my favorite dish. He's got a lot of great food to choose from. I'm sure you'll love what you order."*

Steve Ligidakis

"Chicken Picata!!! ...!
"Exquisite — the lighest chicken breast with a hint of lemon. Bravisima!!!!"

Rita Higdon
Phoenix, AZ

Chicken Picata

1-8 oz. boneless chicken breast
1 stick of butter
1 sm. lemon, cut in half
1/4 cup white cooking wine
1 serving Fettuccini noodles
Flour
1 egg, beaten
1/2 lb. mushrooms, sliced
1/2 sm. zucchini, sliced

Coat chicken with flour, dip in egg and roll again in flour. Melt butter in heavy skillet, add chicken and saute well on both sides 4 to 5 minutes, until brown. Squeeze 1/2 of the lemon on chicken.

Add the mushrooms and zucchini and saute for about 6-7 more minutes. Then add the wine and reduce heat to simmer. Squeeze the other half of the lemon juice into the skillet and simmer for 6-8 minutes longer.

Serve the chicken and sauce over a plate of cooked Fettuccini noodles. Makes 1 serving.

Beggars' Chicken

1/4 cup chopped green
  onions
Dried Lotus leaves or
  dried Bamboo leaves
1 Tbsp. chopped sausage
2 Tbsps. sliced mushrooms
2 Tbsps. chopped walnuts
1/3 cup long grain rice
2 Tbsps. canned Lotus seeds
2 Tbsps. shredded bamboo
  shoots

4 lbs. whole chicken
1/4 cup sherry
3 Tbsps. oil
2 Tbsps. diced ham
1/4 cup sauerkraut
1/8 tsp. cayenne pepper
2 Tbsps. raisins
1/4 cup chicken

Place chicken, sherry and onions in a tight bag and refrigerate overnight, turning occasionally. Soak lotus or bamboo leaves in water for about 1 hour to soften.

Heat oil in a deep, heavy saucepan. Add all of the ingredients except the chicken, rice, lotus seeds and bamboo shoots. Fry for 3-4 minutes. Then add the chicken and rice, cover and cook another 20 minutes. Add the lotus seeds and bamboo shoots, remove from heat, stir and set aside to cool.

Stuff the chicken and top cavity with the rice mixture. Skewer the openings. Wrap with leaves from side to side and lengthwise, wrapping each leaf with string.

Place in a baking dish with a cover, add 1/2" of water or chicken broth. Cover and bake in a 350° oven for about 3-1/2 hours.

If leaves are not available, use aluminum foil. Bake for only 2-1/2 hours, if using aluminum foil.

Cornish Hens Spinaci

2 Cornish hens
1/2 tsp. brandy
2 tsp. olive oil
1 cup fresh spinach,
   chopped
Chopped livers from
   2 Cornish hens
3 strips bacon, sauteed,
   chopped
1/4 cup Riccota cheese

1/8 cup Feta cheese
Juice of 1/2 lemon
Juice of 1 lime
1/2 tsp. oregano
1/2 tsp. thyme
1 tsp. butter
1/4 cup chopped onion
1 tsp. oregano
1/2 tsp. nutmeg
1/2 tsp. black pepper

Wash and dry the 2 hens. Sprinkle the lemon and lime juice into the cavities of the birds. Mix the brandy, olive oil, thyme and 1/2 tsp. of organo, and season the cavities with the mixture.

Heat butter in a skillet and saute onion for 3-4 minutes. Add the spinach and cook for 7-8 more minutes. Then put the chopped Cornish hen livers in the skillet and cook for 3-4 more minutes and remove pan from heat.

Mix the bacon, cheeses, nutmeg, pepper and 1/2 tsp. of oregano in a bowl along with the cooked spinach mixture.

Stuff the hens and skewer the opening. Skewer the legs and wings to the body and place hens in a casserole. Make a sauce of 1 tablespoon of butter and 1/2 cup chicken stock. Use this to baste the birds, and pour the remainder of the stock into the casserole. Cover with aluminum foil.

Bake in a 350° oven for about 1 hour, basting with butter every 15-20 minutes. Remove foil for the final 20 minutes of the cooking.

Apricot Hens

4 Cornish hens. Remove necks and giblets. Discard the necks, and chop the giblets.

2 cups dry white
  breadcrumbs
1 Tbsp. ginger
2 Tbsp. mayonnaise
1 Tbsp. ginger
2 Tbsps. sherry
1/2 cup cooking sherry

Chopped giblets
4 green onions, chopped
1 cup apricot jam
2 Tbsps. soy sauce
1/2 tsp. tabasco
1/2 cup chicen broth

Combine the giblets, onions, 1 tablespoon of the ginger and the breadcrumbs. Use the mixture to stuff the hens, and then secure all openings. Rub hens with the mayonnaise and place in a greased pan. Bake in a 400° oven for about 30 minutes.

Meanwhile boil the tabasco, 2 tablespoons of sherry, the apricot jam, soy sauce and ginger, stirring constantly. Use this sauce to brush hens liberally. Return to the oven and bake for 40 more minutes, basting frequently with the rest of the sauce.

Place hens on a serving plate. Deglaze the pan and add to it 1/2 cup chicen broth and the 1/4 cup of sherry. Boil and pour the contents over the hens, scraping the pan clean.

Turkey Tostada

8 oz. slice cooked turkey
  breast
1/8 cup white cooking wine
5 oz. sliced Provolone cheese
Lightly sauteed zucchini slices

1/2 cup butter
6 mushrooms, sliced
5 oz. sliced ham

Dip turkey in flour. Heat butter in skillet and saute turkey until both sides are brown, 3-4 minutes on each side. Remove turkey and place in a small cooking casserole.

Put mushrooms in the skillet and saute until soft. Add wine to skillet and saute for a minute more and then remove pan from heat. Place ham and then Provolone on top of turkey. Place sauteed mushrooms on top of cheese and bake in 350° oven for about 20 minutes. Garnish with sauteed zucchini.

Makes 1 serving.

Leg of Lamb, the Classic Way

1 leg of lamb, 5 to 6 lbs.
1 Tbsp. oregano
Juice of 2 lemons
24 small potoates, peeled
1/2 cup white wine

1 Tbsp. black pepper
3 garlic cloves, minced
1/2 Tbsp. thyme
1/2 cup olive oil
1 cup butter

Pour oil and lemon juice over lamb. Rub with spices on all sides.Marinate for 6 to 8 hours.

Place lamb in a 350° oven. Melt 1 cup butter and mix with white wine, to use for basting. Brush the lamb occasionally as you bake for 45 minutes.

Add the peeled potatoes to the roasting pan and brush with the butter/wine mix. Bake 1 hour longer. Serves about six.

Leg in Foil

1 leg of lamb, 5 to 6 lbs.
3 coarsely chopped garlic cloves
1/4 lb. Kaseri or Provolone cheese, cubed
2 lbs. pearl onions, peeled, parboiled
Juice of 2 lemons
1 Tbsp. thyme

1Tbsp. pepper
1/2 cup butter
1/2 lb. red onions, sliced
2 Tbsps. parsley, chopped
2 Tbsps. mint, chopped
1/2 cup white wine
1/2 cup olive oil
1 Tbsp. oregano

Rub lamb with pepper. Melt the butter in a skillet and brown the leg, lightly, on all sides. Reserve the cooking butter.

Grease a large double sheet of aluminum foil and place lamb in the center. Make slits in the lamb a few inches apart and place garlic and cheese in the slits.

Use the reserved butter and saute the onions for 3-4 minutes. Add the parsley and mint and saute another 3-4 minutes. Place the onions around the leg of lamb. Mix the wine, olive oil and lemon juice and pour over the lamb. Rub meat with a mixture of oregano and thyme. Fold foil around the meat and seal tightly with string. Roast in a 350° oven for about 2-1/2 hours.

Makes 5 to 6 servings.

Gyros

1/2 lb. ground lamb	1 lb. ground beef
4 Tbsps. minced fresh parsley	1 cup breadcrumbs
2 minced garlic cloves	2 eggs
1 tsp. oregano	1 tsp. cumin
1/2 tsp. black pepper	1 tsp. thyme
Juice of one lemon	1/2 onion, minced

Mix all ingredients well in a bowl. Press mixture into a large log. Wrap with Saran wrap and freeze.

Slice the frozen Gyros in thin slices and grill. Use 6 oz. of meat for each sandwich. Place in the middle of a piece of heated Pita bread. Top with sliced tomatoes, chopped lettuce, chopped onions, and yogurt sauce.

Roman Lamb

8 oz. lamb (not leg) cut into pieces	1/2 cup olive oil
1 large head Romaine lettuce, cut into pieces	6 green onions, chopped
	1/4 cup water
	1 Tbsp. chopped parsley
1 Tbsp. chopped dill	1 tsp. black pepper
1/2 pint whipping cream	1 lemon

Parboil lamb, discard water. Heat olive oil in a deep saucepan and saute lamb 6 to 8 minutes. Add lettuce and onions and saute for 3-4 minutes, until onions are soft. Add water and let boil for 20 minutes.

Add the parsley, dill and pepper, stir, cover, and simmer for 25 minutes. Squeeze the juice from the lemon into the pan and stir thoroughly. Add the whipping cream and stir. Let simmer 5-6 more minutes. Makes 1 serving.

"The food here is always excellent — superior to any of the other restaurants in the Valley."

Ellen Wilcox

Feta Lamb Chops

1 lamb chop, about 8 oz.
1 small red onion,
  thinly sliced
2 artichoke hearts, broken
4 oz. whole tomatoes in
  juice, crushed
3 oz. Feta cheese, crumbled

1/4 cup olive oil
1 small onion, thinly sliced
2 cloves of chopped garlic
1 tsp. mint leaves
1 tsp. oregano
Black pepper, to taste

Heat olive oil in a heavy skillet. Dip chop in flour and then brown well on both sides. Add onion, artichoke hearts and garlic and saute for 3 to 4 minutes. Add the crushed tomatoes, mint leaves, oregano and black pepper. Reduce heat and cook for 6 to 8 minutes. Add the Feta cheese, stirring in until the cheese melts. Makes 1 serving.

Celery Heart Pork

1 center cut pork chop, 8 oz.
1 small onion, thinly sliced
1 whole artichoke heart,
  sliced and marinated
1/4 cup white cooking wine
1/4 pint whipping cream

1/4 cup olive oil
1/2 lemon
2 cloves chopped garlic
Black pepper
1 egg yolk

Heat olive oil in a skillet and brown pork chop well on both sides. Squeeze in the juice from the lemon. Add the onion, artichoke heart and garlic and saute for 4-5 minutes. Add the wine and pepper and cook for 3-4 minutes more.

Remove the pork cho. Put the whipping cream in the skillet and stir well for 2 minutes over low heat. Stir in the egg yolk, cooking for another minute.

Cover the pork chop with the sauce. Makes 1 serving.

"My aim at Golden Cuisine is to have everything on the menu at least once. It's going to be very difficult when I get the Veal Skordato every time."

Gerri DuRoss

Veal Stefano

2 veal slices, about
3 oz. each
4 thin slices of eggplant
2 whole artichoke hearts,
broken
1 large ripe tomato,
chopped
1 tsp. cinnamon

Pepper, to taste
1/4 cup olive oil
1 clove chopped garlic
1/4 cup red cooking
wine
1/2 tsp. nutmeg
1 tsp. parsley

Dip veal in flour. Saute in olive oil in heavy skillet until lightly brown on both sides. Remove meat.

Place eggplant, artichoke hearts, garlic and tomato in the skillet and saute until eggplant is soft. Add the wine and spices, reduce heat and cook for 4 to 5 minutes.

Place 1 veal fillet in a cooking casserole. Spoon the sauce in, cover with the other slice of veal. Sprinkle with 4 oz. of shredded Mozzarella cheese and bake 20-25 minutes in a 350° oven.

Veal Skordato

2 thin slices of veal,
about 3 oz. each
1 Tbsp. sliced almonds
1 Tbsp. chopped walnut
Dry breadcrumbs
3 oz. shredded Provolone
2 oz. shredded Mozzarella

3 oz. ham, chopped
2 cloves chopped garlic
Flour
1 egg, beaten
1/2 cup butter
1/2 cup whipping cream

Place 1 veal slice on a working surface. Put ham and garlic in the middle, and cover with the 2nd slice. Dip veal in flour.

Mix egg and nuts and coat veal with mixture, then roll the meat well in dry breadcrumbs. Melt butter in skillet and brown veal on both sides, 4-5 minutes to a side. Place meat in a small cooking casserole. Heat whipping cream and cheese over low burner until cheese is melted. Pour sauce over veal and bake in 350° oven for 15-20 minutes. Garnish with a few sauteed zucchini slices. Makes 1 serving.

Baby Corn Steak

8 oz. tenderloin steak,
in chunks
1 sm. chopped sweet red
pepper
1 sm. green bell pepper,
thinly sliced
1/8 cup white cooking wine
1/4 tsp. chili powder

1/4 cup whipping cream
1/4 cup vegetable oil
6 baby corn
1/2 onion, thinly sliced
1 green onion, chopped
2 cloves chopped garlic
Black pepper, to taste

Heat oil in skillet and saute steak until light brown on both sides. Add corn, onion, peppers and garlic and saute until all vegetables are soft. Reduce heat and pour in cooking wine, stir well and cook for 4-5 minutes. Add the black pepper and chili powder, stir thoroughly, and then stir in the whipping cream, remove from heat and serve. Makes 1 serving.

Steak Stefado

10 oz. tenderloin steak,
cubed
2 cloves of garlic, chopped
1/4 cup red cooking wine
1 tsp. Rosemary
1 tsp. black pepper
2 cinnamon sticks
1/4 tsp. nutmeg

1/2 cup olive oil
1 onion, thinly sliced
4 oz. whole tomatoes,
in juice, crushed
2 bay leaves
6 whole peppercorns
1/4 tsp. cinnamon

Heat olive oil in a skillet. Saute steak for about 2 minutes on each side. Add onion and saute until they are soft. Then add garlic and saute for another 2-3 minutes. Reduce heat and pour the red wine and crushed tomatoes with juice into the skillet. Then add all the spices, cover, and simmer for 20 minutes over low heat. Makes 1 serving.

Pepper Steak

One 8 oz. fillet mignon
1/4 cup red cooking wine
1 Tbsp. black olives, sliced
1 Tbsp. sliced green olives
1 tsp. Worchestershire sauce
1 small tomato, cubed
1 Tbsp. steak sauce
Cooked Fettuccini noodles

1 cup olive oil
1 green pepper
1/2 red pepper
1 small onion
1/2 red onion
6 mushrooms
1 tsp. soy sauce

Heat olive oil in a heavy skillet and saute for steak for about 5 minutes. Add the red wine and reduce heat. Slice all the vegetables thinly and add to the skillet. Saute until soft. Add the olives and the steak, soy and Worchestershire sauces and stir well. Saute for 4 to 5 more minutes. Put the cubed tomato in the skillet and cook for another 1-2 minutes. Then serve over Fettuccini noodles. Makes 1 serving.

Steak Metaxa

8 oz. filet mignon steak,
  butterflied
1/4 cup green onions,
  chopped
1/4 cup white onion,
  chopped
1/4 oz. cooking sherry
Black pepper, to taste

1 Tbsp. Dijon mustard
1/4 cup olive oil
1/4 cup vegetable oil
1/2 Metaxa brandy
1/2 tsp. grated orange peel
1/2 cup whipping cream
1/2 tsp. grated nutmeg

Heat olive and vegetable oil in a heavy skillet and saute the steak for 5 to 6 minutes on each side, over medium heat. Add the onions and saute until they are soft. Pour the brandy and orange peel into the skillet, then the sherry. Stir well. Remove steak and place on a serving plate.

Add the whipping cream, nutmeg, pepper and mustard to the skillet. Stir over low heat for about 5 minutes, then pour this sauce over the steak. Makes 1 serving.

Calamari Capellini

1 lb. Calamari,
   cut into pieces
4 green onions, chopped
2 cloves garlic, chopped
5 peppercorns
3 cloves
1/2 lb. cooked Capellini
1/2 tsp. black pepper

1/4 cup olive oil
1/8 cup dry white wine
2 tomatoes, cubed
1/2 Tbsps. pepper flakes
1 Tbsp. chopped parsley
2 bay leaves
1 tsp. basil

Heat olive oil in heavy skillet and fry Calamari until soft, or for about 3 to 4 minutes. Add the white wine to the skillet, then the onion and garlic and saute for 1-2 minutes. Spoon the sauce over the cooked Capellini. Makes 2 servings.

Scallops Plaki

10 deep sea scallops
1/2 onion, sliced thin
1 small carrot, chopped
1/8 cup white wine
1 tsp. basil
1/8 tsp. black pepper
1 Tbsp. bland raisins

1/2 cup olive oil
Flour
1 lg. tomato, peeled, sliced
1 clove garlic, chopped
1 tsp. parsley
1/8 tsp. sugar
1 Tbsp. pine nuts

Heat olive oil in heavy skillet and saute scallops for 4 to 5 minutes. Add the onion and carrot and saute for another 2-3 minutes; then the tomato and garlic for yet another 2-3 minutes. Pour in the white wine and reduce heat to low. Stir in the basil, parsley, sugar and pepper and cook for 8 to 10 minutes.

Finally, add the pine nuts and raisins and stir thoroughly. Remove from heat and serve.

Feta Shrimp

1/2 onion, thinly sliced	1/4 cup oil
6 green onions, chopped	1 clove garlic, chopped
4 oz. whole tomatoes, in juice	1/8 cup white wine
1 Tbsp. parsley, chopped	1/2 tsp. black pepper
1 tsp. oregano	1 tsp. thyme
1/2 tsp. rosemary	1 tsp. basil
1 Tbps. grated Romano chese	1/4 cup butter
	1/2 lemon
6 oz. small bay shrimp	

Heat oil in skillet and saute the onions and garlic until soft. Pour the wine into the skillet, then crush the tomatoes and add them plus the tomato juice to the skillet. Stir in the spices and grated Romano and cook for 4 to 5 minutes.

In a separate skillet, heat the butter and saute the shrimp for 4 to 5 minutes. Squeeze in the juice from the 1/2 lemon. Now add the shrimp to the sauce mix and place the entire recipe into a small casserole. Sprinkle 1/4 lb. of crumbled Feta cheese over the sauce. Bake in a 375° oven for 20 to 25 minutes.

"Our daughter Hailaine recommended your restaurant to us and said, 'When you come out to Phoenix you have to eat at this place called the Golden Cusine'. *She was absolutely right. Your food is delicious, and we'll be here again whenever we get to Phoenix."*

Toby and Ed Gordon
Hoffman Estates, Illinois

Marine Scallops

12 oz. scallops	1/2 cup butter
2 cloves garlic, chopped	2 Tbsps. sherry
1/2 cup cracker crumbs	3 Tbsps. butter
Pepper, to taste	1 tsp. parsley

Place scallops in a greased baking dish. Pour 1/2 cup melted butter and sherry over the scallops. Sprinkle scallops with chopped garlic and pepper. Bake 20 minutes in a 350° oven. Top the scallops with a mixture of the cracker crumbs, parsley and 3 tablespoons of melted butter, and bake 5 more minutes. Makes 2 servings.

Smelts Milanese

1/2 lb. clean smelt	Flour
1/2 lemon	1/2 cup oil
1/4 cup vegetable oil	1/2 onion, thinly sliced
4 oz. whole tomatoes, in juice, crushed	2 cloves garlic, chopped
	2 Tbps. tomato puree
1 tsp. oregano	Pepper, to taste
1 tsp. parsley	1 tsp. thyme
4 oz. shredded Mozzarella	1 Tbps. grated Romano

Coat smelt with flour and fry in 1/2 cup oil, until they are well browned. Squeeze juice from 1/2 lemon over the smelt. Then place the fish in a small cooking casserole.

Heat 1/4 cup vegetable oil in a skillet. Saute the onions and garlic until soft, then add tomatoes and juice and saute for another 3 to 4 minutes.

Add the tomato puree, pepper, oregano, parsley and thyme, stirring well, and saute 3 to 4 minutes. Spoon this sauce over the smelt and sprinkle the grated Romano and Mozzarella cheese over the top. Bake in a 375° oven for 20-25 minutes.

Scrod Broccoli

One 8 oz. fillet of scrod	Flour
1/2 cup frying oil	1 egg, beaten
1-1/2 cup broccoli flowerettes, chopped coarsely	1/2 red bell pepper, thinly sliced
1/2 cup white wine	1/2 onion, sliced thinly
1/4 pint whipping cream	Pepper, to taste

Roll scrod in flour, dip into beaten egg and roll again in the flour. Brown well on both sides in the frying oil. Add the broccoli, bell pepper and onion and saute for 3 to 4 minutes. Pour the white wine in the skillet and pepper, to taste. Saute another 2-3 minutes. Add the whipping cream and stir well. Simmer over a low heat for 4-5 minutes, and serve.

Shrimp Athena

4 large shrimp	Flour
4 green onions, chopped	1 egg, beaten
1/2 onion, thinly sliced	1 cup butter
2 cloves of garlic	1/2 lemon
1/8 cup white cooking wine	1 tsp. oregano
4 oz. can of whole tomatoes, in juice, crushed	1 tsp. thyme
	1 tsp. basil
Pepper, to taste	1 Tbsp. parlsey
1 Tbsp. grated Parmesan cheese	1/2 tsp. rosemary

Peel, clean and butterfly the shrimp, then roll each in flour, dip into the beaten egg, and roll a second time in the flour. Melt 1/2 cup of the butter in a skillet and saute shrimp until golden brown. Squeeze in the juice from the half lemon. Now place the shrimp in a small baking dish.

Heat the other 1/2 cup of butter in a saucepan. Saute the onions and garlic until soft. Reduce heat and pour the wine into the saucepan, then the tomatoes and juice, and stir well. Finally add the other spices and saute for 8-10 minutes. Spoon this sauce over the shrimp, and bake int a 350° oven for 20-25 minutes. Makes 1 serving.

Coconut Fried Shrimp

4 large shrimp	Flour
Shredded coconut	1 egg, beaten
Oil for deep frying	Cocktail sauce
	Dash of pineapple juice

Clean, wash and devein the shrimp. Roll in flour, then dip in beaten egg and coat thoroughly with shredded coconut.

Heat the oil at 375° in a deep fryer and cook shrimp until golden brown. Serve them with cocktail sauce which has been mixed with a little bit of pineapple juice.

Artichoke Sole

One 5 oz. fillet of sole
2 whole artichoke hearts,
   crushed
4 green onions, chopped
1/4 cup white cooking wine
1/4 pint whipping cream

1 egg yolk
Flour
1 egg, beaten
1/4 cup butter
5 mushrooms, sliced
Pepper, to taste

Coat sole with flour, dip in beaten egg and roll again in the flour. Melt butter in a saucepan and brown sole on both sides, 2-3 minutes on each side.

Add onions, mushrooms and artichoke hearts to saucepan and saute for 5 to 6 minutes. Stir in the wine and pepper and saute for another 3-4 minutes, then thoroughly stir in the whipping cream while reducing heat to low. Cook over the low heat for about 2 or 3 minutes. Remove sole and place it in a serving dish. Place the egg yolk in the saucepan, stir continuously for two minutes. Pour sauce over the sole. Makes 1 serving.

Corinthian Sea Bass

One 6 oz. sea bass fillet
1/2 small onion, chopped
2 cloves of garlic, chopped
1/8 cup white cooking wine
4 oz. whole tomatoes, in
   juice, crushed
1/2 tsp. oregano

2 Tbsps. vegetable oil
4 Tbsps. olive oil
Flour
1 Tbsp. sliced black olives
1 tsp. parsley
1/2 tsp. whole resoemar
Pepper, to taste

Heat vegetable and olive oil in a heavy skillet. Coat sea bass well with flour and brown evenly on both sides.

Add the onion, garlic and olives and saute for two minutes, then stir in the wine, tomatoes and juice, and the spices. Cook for 10-12 minutes. Makes 1 serving.

Calamari Provencale

6 small squid, cleaned
1 cup sliced mushrooms
2 cloves of garlic, chopped
6 green onions, chopped
1/8 cup white cooking wine
1 tsp. thyme
1/2 tsp. oregano
1 Tbsp. grated Romano
cheese
1/2 Tbsp. grated Parmesan
cheese

1/4 cup frying oil
1 egg, beaten
1/2 lemon
1/2 cup butter
2 tomatoes, chopped
1 tsp. parsley
1/2 tsp. basil
1/2 tsp. rosemary
Pepper, to taste

Coat squid with flour, dip in egg batter and again roll in the flour. Heat frying oil in skillet and cook squid until well browned. Squeeze the juice from the half-lemon over the squid and then remove from heat. Place squid in a small cooking casserole.

Melt the butter in a saucepan and saute the mushrooms, garlic, onions and tomatoes until soft, for about 6-8 minutes. Stir in the wine and reduce the heat. Add the spices and the cheese and saute 4-5 more minutes.

Pour sauce over squid and bake in a 350° oven for about 20 minutes. Makes 1 serving.

"When we die and go to heaven we are going to be allowed to do things we liked to enjoy here on Earth. So, I hope Nick enjoys cooking Stuffed Zucchini as much as I like to eat it.

"I come to Nick's restaurant at least once a week, but usually reguarly 3 times a week."

Melva

Stuffed Zucchini

1 med. zucchini squash	1/2 cup Feta cheese, crumbled
2 cloves of garlic, chopped	1 stick butter
1/4 cup red cooking wine	1 small onion, chopped
1 Tbsp. grated Romano cheese	1/2 lb. ground beef
	1 tsp. oregano
1 tsp. grated Parmesan cheese	1 tsp. thyme
	1 tsp. parsley
Pinch of black pepper	1 cup Riccota cheese
1/2 pulp of zucchini, chopped	

Discard ends of the zucchini. Cut in half crosswise and boil until tender. Cut in half again lengthwise. Scoop out pulp and set aside. Place zucchini shell in a baking dish with hollow ends facing up. Discard half of the pulp.

Saute onion and garlic in butter until soft, 3-4 minutes. Add the ground beef and saute until browned. Add the wine, then the spices, grated cheese and zucchini pulp and saute for 3 to 4 more minutes.

Place this mixture on top of the zucchini shells. Top with the Riccota cheese, spread evenly, and crumble the Feta cheese atop the Riccota. Bake in a 375° oven for 25 to 30 minutes, or until cheese is brown on top.

Stuffed Eggplant

1 medium eggplant
1/2 onion, thinly sliced
1 clove garlic, minced
1 tomato, peeled, chopped
1 Tbsp. grated Romano cheese

Oil for frying
1/8 cup more oil
1/4 lb. ground beef
1 Tbsp. parsley
Pepper, to taste

Cut eggplant in half lengthwise, scoop out the seeds. Brown both halves lightly in a skillet with a bit of cooking oil, then drain the eggplant on paper towels and place it in a small baking casserole, hollow side up.

Heat the 1/8 cup oil in a saucepan and saute the onion and garlic until the onions are soft. Add the ground beef and saute until evenly brown. Finally add the tomato, parsley, pepper and Romano and saute for about 4-5 more minutes. Spoon this mixture into the eggplant shells. Sprinkle about 4 oz. of grated Mozzarella cheese on top. Bake in a 375° oven for 25 minutes.

Eggplant Mousaka

1/2 lb. potatoes, peeled, sliced
1/2 tsp. nutmeg
1/4 lb. eggplant, thinly sliced
2 green onions, chopped
1/8 cup red cooking wine
1 large red ripe tomato
1 tsp. grated Parmesan
1 tsp. grated Romano

*6 oz. shredded Mozzarella
1/4 cup vegetable oil
1/2 onion, thinly sliced
1 clove of garlic, chopped
4 mushrooms, sliced
1/4 lb. ground beef
Pepper, to taste
1 tsp. oregano
1/2 tsp. cinnamon
1 tsp. parsley

Heat oil in a skillet and fry sliced potatoes until they are brown. Add eggplant and continue to cook until soft. Remove the eggplant and potato and drain. Then use the same skillet to saute the onion, garlic, mushrooms and ground beef until onions are soft and the meat is brown. Add the wine and cubed tomatoes, stir well and saute for 5 minutes. Then add spices and grated cheeses and cook another 3-4 minutes. Place half of this sauce in a cooking dish, layer with eggplant and potatoes, pour rest of the sauce on top, sprinkle with Mozzarella and bake in a 375° oven for 25-30 minutes.

*You can substitute shredded Kaseri cheese for one-half of the Mozzarella, if available.

Stuffed Grapevine Leaves

4 dz. grapevine leaves
6 green onions, chopped
1 Tbsp. fresh parsley,
  chopped
1/2 cup raisins
1 cup white wine
Juice from 1/2 lemon
3 Tbsps. yogurt sauce

3 Tbsps. olive oil
1 Tbsp. fresh dill, chopped
3/4 cup rice
1/2 cup pine nuts
Pepper, to taste
1 Tbsp. olive oil
Beef stock

Remove grape leaves from jar and rinse in hot water. Place one leaf on working surface. Put second leaf on top of the first, overlapping almost half way. Place 1 tablespoon of stuffing (below) on the bottom of the first leaf, roll to cover the stuffing, fold the ends, and then roll tightly.

STUFFING:

Heat 3 tablespoons of olive oil in a skillet. Saute the onions, parsley and dill about 2-3 minutes and reduce heat. Add the rice, pine nuts, raisins, wine and pepper and simmer for about 15 minutes, stirring frequently.

Grease bottom of a soup kettle with 1 tablespoon of olive oil. Arrange stuffed and rolled graveleaves in the kettle. Sprinkle the top with a mixture of lemon juice, olive oil, beef stock and pepper. Then put second layer of grape leaves over the top. Repeat until all grape leaves are in the kettle.

Place a weight (a plate works best) on top of the grape leaves. Add water, to the top of the leaves, and simmer for 50 to 60 minutes. Add water if necessary during cooking.

Allow to cool before removing. Place 4 grape leaves in a small casserole, top with 3 tablespoons of yogurt sauce, sprinkle with about a tablespoon of pine nuts, and bake in a 350° oven for 15 to 20 minutes. Makes 2 dozen grape leaves, or 6 servings.

Eggplant Parmigiana

2 thin eggplant slices
2 cups oil for frying
1 Tbsp. grated Parmesan
1 Tbsp. grated Romano
4 oz. shredded Mozzarella

Flour
1 egg, beaten
bread crumbs
2 cups meat sauce

Roll eggplant in flour, dip in beaten egg, and coat with breadcrumbs. Heat oil in skillet and saute eggplant until brown on both sides.

Please 1/2 meat sauce in a cooking casserole. Place the eggplant over the sauce. Sprinkle grated cheese over top, pour 2nd cup of meat sauce over the eggplant, and top with the shredded Mozzarella. Bake at 350° for about 25 to 30 minutes.

> *"Nick's Golden Cuisine is much, much more than a restaurant. It's the best parts of home, with great food and huge portions.*
>
> *"Nick is a host who knows you as a good friend and who offers prices so low you overtip to ward off guilt. Each dish is assembled fresh as you wait, flavorful and wonderful. Having eaten twice my growing weight in 'golden fare', I can only plead addiction as my excuse."*
>
> **Steve Roberts**

Stuffed Potato Skins

4 large pototoes, cut in half   1 cup frying oil

Scoop out the meat of the potatoes, leaving thick skin shells. Heat oil in a skillet and fry the potato skins until they are light brown. Then fill with various stuffings, as follows:

Spinach Skins

3/4 lb. chopped, cooked
   spinach
4 Tbsps. Riccota cheese

1/2 lb. Feta cheese
1 tsp. chopped dill

Put 4 potato skins in a shallow baking dish. Mix spinach, Feta cheese and dill and spoon filling into the skins. Spoon Ricotta over each skin, and bake in 375° oven until cheese is lightly browned; 15 to 20 minutes. Serve with yogurt sauce.

Bacon Skins

8 strips of fried bacon   4 potato skins
6 oz. shredded mild
  cheddar cheese

Place two strips of bacon on each potato skin. Place in a shallow baking dish. Sprinkle shredded mild cheddar cheese on top of the skins, and bake in a 375° oven until the cheese is melted, or for about 10 to 15 minutes.

Turkey Skins

6 oz. cooked turkey breast,   4 potato skins
  sliced   1/8 cup butter
5 oz. shredded Mozzarella   1 cup sliced mushrooms

Place skins in a shallow baking dish. Heat butter in skillet and saute mushrooms and turkey until lightly brown. Spoon the meat and mushrooms into the skins and top with the Mozzarella cheese. Bake in a 375° oven for 15 to 20 minutes, or until cheese is lightly brown. Serve with yogurt sauce.

Western Skins

1 cup green peppers, sliced   4 potato skins
4 oz. sliced ham   1/2 cup butter
4 oz. mild cheddar cheese   1 onion, sliced

Put skins in a shallow baking dish. Heat butter in a heavy skillet and saute ham, peppers and onion until vegetables are soft. Spoon filling into the potato skins, top with shredded cheddar cheese. Bake in a 375° oven for 15 to 20 minutes, or until cheese is well melted. Serve with sour cream.

Chicken Wings

New York Style

12 chicken wings
1/4 tsp. hot chili flakes
1/2 tsp. thyme
1 tsp. parsley

1 cup B.B.Q. sauce
1/2 tsp. black pepper
1 tsp. oregano
1/2 tsp. basil

Place chicken wings in a baking casserole. Pour the B.B.Q. sauce over the wings, and sprinkle top with mixture of all the spices. Bake in a 375° oven for 25 to 30 minutes.

Greek Style

12 chicken wings
1 tsp. parsley
1 tsp. oregano
1/2 tsp. black pepper
1/4 cup melted butter

Juice of 1 lemon
1 clove garlic, chopped
1 tsp. basil
1 tsp. thyme

Place wings in a baking casserole. Squeeze lemon juice over the fowl, then sprinkle top with mixture of the spices and the garlic. Pour melted butter over the wings and bake in a 350° oven for 25 to 30 minutes.

Honey Dipped

8 chicken wings
Buttermilk pancake mix
(see page 1)
1 tsp. cinnamon

Oil for frying
Flour
1 cup honey
1/8 cup water

Coat wings with flour, dip in pancake batter and roll again in the flour. Heat oil in a skillet and fry wings until golden brown.

Mix honey, water and cinnamon well. Dip each wing in the honey sauce to coat thoroughly with the mixture. Serve.

7

Sauces and Dressings

Pizza Sauce

4 cloves of garlic, chopped
1 #10 can of tomato puree
1 #10 can whole tomatoes
   in juice
1/2 cup black pepper
1/4 cup beef stock
1/8 cup grated Romano
   cheese

1 cup butter
2 onions, chopped
1 cup oregano
1/2 cup basil
1/2 cup chicken stock
1/4 cup dill
1/4 cup thyme

Melt butter in a large pot. Add the onions and garlic and cook over low heat until soft. Add the tomato puree to the pot and then fill the #10 can one-quarter full of water. Add this to the sauce. Crush tomatoes and put them in the pot. Then add the spices and stir well. Simmer for 5 to 6 hours, stirring occasionally. Refrigerate. This sauce holds good for about two to three weeks.

Meat Sauce

4 cloves of garlic, chopped
1 cup of mushrooms, sliced
1 celery stalk, chopped
1-1/2 lbs. lean ground beef
1 #10 can tomato puree
1 #10 can tomatoes, in
juice, crushed
1 Tbsp. grated Romano
1/4 cup chicken stock

1 cup butter
2 onions, chopped
1/4 cup bay leaves
1 small carrot, chopped
1 Tbsp. oregano
2 Tbsps. basil
1 Tbsp. thyme
1 Tbsp. black pepper
1/2 cup beef stock

Melt butter in a large pot. Saute the onions, garlic, mushrooms, bay leaves, celery and carrot until onions are soft.

Add the ground beef and saute until beef is brown. Then add the tomato puree, along with enough water to fill one-quarter of the #10 can. Stir in the crushed tomatoes and juice.

Finally, add the spices, grated cheese, and the chicken and beef stock. Stir well and simmer for three to four hours.

This sauce freezes well.

> **"Anyone who hasn't tried Nick's** Gyros Sandwich **is truly missing out on quite a taste experience. The** Yogurt Sauce **is the special touch that tops it off.**
>
> **Pamela Awe**

Yogurt Dressing

1-1/2 cups mayonnaise
1/2 cup cucumber, chopped,
peeled and seeded
1 Tbsp. grated Romano
cheese
1 Tbsp. grated Parmesan
cheese

1/2 tsp. sugar
1 cup sour cream
1 cup plain yogurt
2 green onions, chopped
Juice of 1 lemon
1 tsp. Dijon mustard
1/2 tsp. black pepper

Mix all ingredients well. Chill before serving. Makes about 5 cups of Yogurt Dressing.

Ranch Style Dressing

2 cups mayonnaise
2 cloves of garlic, minced
1 tsp. Worchestershire
sauce
Dash of tabasco

1 cup sour cream
1 cup buttermilk
2 tsps. black pepper
1 tsp. Dijon mustard

Mix well, chill and serve.

Bleu Cheese

2 cups mayonnaise
1 clove garlic, minced
1 cup crumbled bleu cheese
1 tsp. Worchestershire
sauce

1 cup sour cream
1 cup buttermilk
1 tsp. black pepper
1 tsp. Dijon mustard

Mix well, chill and serve.

Feta Cheese Dressing

2-1/2 cups Feta cheese,
crumbled
3/4 cup red wine vinegar
2 tsps. oregano
3 Tbsps. olive oil

1/2 tsp. black pepper
3 cups mayonnaise
2 garlic cloves, minced
1 tsp. thyme
1 tsp. basil

Mix all ingredients thoroughly. Chill and serve.

"The Golden Cuisine is one of the best restaurants I've ever visited. I've enjoyed every entree' I've tried. I especially loved the Feta Cheese Dressing. I'm looking forward to my next visit to Phoenix and to Nick's Golden Cuisine."

Stacy H. Lindbergh
Charleston, S.C.

Thousand Island Dressing

1 quart mayonnaise
1/2 cup diced onions
3 hard boiled eggs, chopped
1 tsp. Worchestershire sauce
1/4 cup diced pimentoes

8 oz. dill relish
12 oz. chili sauce
1/2 tsp. black pepper
1 clove of garlic, minced
1/2 tsp. tabasco

Mix all ingredients well. Chill and serve.

Italian Dressing

4 cups vegetable oil
Juice of 1 lemon
1 clove of garlic, minced
1 tsp. basil
1 Tbsp. grated Parmesan cheese
1/2 tsp. black pepper
1/2 tsp. dill weed

1 cup red wine vinegar
1/2 cup pickle juice
1 tsp. oregano
1 tsp. thyme
1 tsp. parsley
1 Tbsp. minced onions
1/2 tsp. rosemary

Mix well. Be sure to shake thoroughly before using each time.

Cheddar Cheese Dressing

1 cup shredded cheddar
  cheese
1 tsp. red wine vinegar
Few drops of
  Worchestershire sauce

4 strips of fried bacon, chopped
2 cups mayonnaise
1 cup buttermilk
Black pepper, to taste
Red pepper, to taste

Mix all ingredients well. Makes 3 cups of dressing.

Vinaigrette

1/4 cup red wine vinegar
1/2 tsp. chopped green
  pepper
1/2 tsp. chopped pimentoes
Dash of sugar

1 egg, lightly beaten
1 cup olive oil
1 tsp. chopped onion
1 Tbsp. Dijon mustard
Pinch of black pepper

Mix all ingredients. Be sure to shake well before each use.

Pesto

4 Tbsps. sweet butter
1 handful fresh basil
  leaves
1/4 cup grated Parmesan
  cheese

Pepper, to taste
3 cloves of garlic
1/4 cup olive oil
1/4 cup pine nuts
1/4 cup walnuts, chopped

Place ingredients in a blender. Mix until thick and creamy.

Variations:

Add 5 medium anchovies to the basic Pesto sauce (above).

Barbeque Sauce

2 onions, finely chopped
1-1/2 tsp. finely chopped
  ginger
17 oz. can whole tomatoes,
  in juice, crushed
Dash of cayenne pepper
1 Tbsp. chili powder
1/2 tsp. oregano
1 tsp. B.B.Q. spice

2 Tbsps. olive oil
3 cloves of garlic, minced
1-1/4 cup chili sauce
1/4 cup dark brown sugar
1/3 cup sherry
1/3 cup soy sauce
1 Tbsp. horseradish
1 tsp. paprika

Heat olive oil in saucepan and cook onions over medium heat for 2 to 3 minutes. Add the garlic, ginger and crushed tomatoes and cook for 3-4 minutes more, bringing to a gentle boil.

Add the rest of the ingredients, stir well, and simmer for about 45 minutes.

"What Nick does with a meal! Makes eating a delight.

"Every meal is a special occasion. Nick is a true artist in his own right. Thank you, Nick. Your friendship and your food I will not forget."

Gilbert A. Soto

Marinara

1 onion, thinly sliced
5 oz. whole tomatoes,
  in juice, crushed
1 tsp. basil
1 tsp. grated Romano
  cheese
1 tsp. grated Parmesan

1/4 cup olive oil
2 cloves garlic, chopped
1 tsp. oregano
1 tsp. thyme
1/2 tsp. black pepper
1 tsp. parsley

Heat olive oil in saucepan and saute onions and garlic until onions are soft, about 2 to 3 minutes. Stir in the crushed tomatoes and juice and continue to saute for 2-3 minutes longer.

Add the spices and grated cheese, reduce heat to medium and cook for 5 to 6 minutes. Makes about 3 cups.

Cocktail Sauce

1 cup chili sauce
2 Tbsps. horseradish
Pinch of pepper
2 Tbsps. finely chopped
  onions

1/8 cup lime juice
Juice of 1 lemon
1/2 tsp. tabasco
1/2 tsp. celery salt

Mix all ingredients well. Makes about 2 cups.

Tartar Sauce

1 cup of mayonnaise
2 Tbsps. chopped green
  onions
1/4 cup chopped green olives
1 Tbsp. red pimentoes,
  chopped

Juice of 1 lemon
2 Tbsps. dill relish
1/4 tsp. dill weed
1/4 tsp. black pepper

Mix well. Makes about 2 cups.

Mustard Sauce

1/2 cup mayonnaise
1 Tbsp. horseradish
Pinch of black pepper

1/2 cup sour cream
3 Tbsps. Dijon mustard

Mix well and chill. Makes 1 cup of sauce.

Eggplant Dip

2 medium eggplants
1 tomato, peeled, chopped
1 tsp. marjoram
1/2 tsp. oregano
1/2 tsp. thyme
3 Tbsps. olive oil

2 cloves of garlic
1 onion, grated
1 Tbsp. parsley
1/2 tsp. basil
1/8 tsp. black pepper

Pierce eggplants and bake for about 1 hour in a 350° oven. Peel and chop the eggplants when done.

Put eggplants and all other ingredients in a blender and run until smooth. Serves about 4.

Tarama Avocado

8 slices of white bread
1 small potato, boiled,
   peeled and chopped
1/2 small avocado, chopped

8 oz. tarama fish roe
3 Tbsps. grated onions
1 cup olive oil
Juice of 2 lemons

Soak bread in water, and then squeeze dry. Place cooked potato in a blender and mix at low speed until smooth. Add the fish roe, onions and avocado, along with the bread, and blend until smooth.

Slowly add the olive oil and lemon juice and turn the blender to high speed until the mixture is creamy. Makes 4 to 5 cups.

Rice Pilaf

1/2 stick butter
1-1/2 lbs. fresh, sliced
   mushrooms
4 cups of chicken broth
1 tsp. oregano
1 tsp. thyme
1 cup white wine

1 onion, finely sliced
3 cloves garlic, chopped
1/4 cup parsley
2 cups of rice
1 tsp. basil
1 tsp. black pepper

Saute onions, mushrooms, garlic and parsley in butter until onions are soft, or for about 6 to 7 minutes. Add the rest of the ingredients and cover. Simmer for 20 minutes over a medium fire.

All of the specialties in this cookbook are SALT FREE!

Meat Balls

2 lbs. ground beef
1 Tbsp. finely chopped onion
2 cloves of garlic, minced
1/4 cup parsley
1 tsp. black pepper

2 eggs
1 cup bread crumbs
1/8 cup milk
1 Tbsp. mint leaves
1/2 tsp. cinnamon

Mix all items thoroughly in a large bowl. Form into small balls, and bake in a 350° oven for about 25 to 30 minutes.

"Each new dish we try is an adventure! It's hard to leave room for one of Nick's excellent desserts!"

Larry and Sandy Morse

"Enjoy!"

Nick ponders his craft.

8

Desserts and Breads

Baklava

1 lb. melted sweet butter	1 lb. Fillo dough
1 cup sugar	1 lb. chopped almonds
2 Tbsps. cinnamon	2 lbs. chopped walnuts
9" x 13" baking pan	

Brush pan with some of the melted butter. Lay one-half of the dough in the bottom of the pan, brushing each leaf with butter and allowing the dough to slightly overlap the edge of the pan.

Mix the nuts, sugar and cinnamon well. Spread as a filling evenly into the pan. Fold the overlapping Fillo over the top of the filling. Lay the rest of the Fillo on top of the filling, brushing every sheet with butter and overlapping each leaf slightly. Work quickly so the Fillo will not dry out. Tuck in the ends of the Fillo.

With a sharp knife, cut the top Fillo layers diagonally to make diamond shaped pieces. Bake in a 350° oven for an hour to an hour and 15 minutes, or until golden brown on top. Makes 24 pieces.

Syrup

4 cups water	2 cups sugar
4 cinnamon sticks	3 cups honey
6 whole cloves	1 Tbsp. cinnamon
1 tsp. grated lemon peel	1/2 whole lemon
1 tsp. grated orange peel	1 tsp. vanilla extract

Bring to boil, simmer about 1 hour. Cool. Spoon syrup over the Baklava and allow to cool several hours before serving.

Kataifi

Begin by making syrup like the one for Baklava on page 102.

2 lbs. coarsely chopped walnuts	1 lb. sweet butter
1/2 lbs. chopped almonds	1/2 cup sugar
1 lb. shredded dough	2 Tbsps. cinnamon
	1/8 cup syrup

Mix nuts, sugar, cinnamon and syrup in a bowl. Brush a baking sheet with butter. Lay a strip of dough, about 3-inches wide and 8-inches long on a floured working surface. Place one heaping tablespoon of the nut mixture in the dough end closest to you. Roll tightly. Place in the baking sheet.

Repeat until all the dough is used. Bake in a 350° oven for about 1 hour, or until brown on top. Pour cooled syrup on top, and let cool for a few hours before serving.

Nut Cake

1/2 lb. softened butter	1 cup sugar
1-1/2 cups chopped walnuts	6 eggs
1-1/2 cups sliced almonds	1 cup flour
2 tsp. grated orange peel	1 cup farina
1 tsp. baking powder	1 tsp. cinnamon

Cream butter with sugar, add eggs and mix well. Add the rest of the ingredients and mix thoroughly. Pour batter into a 13" x 9" buttered pan. Bake at 350° for 30 to 35 minutes.

Syrup

3 cups water	2 cups sugar
2 cinnamon sticks	1 tsp. cinnamon
1/2 lemon	1/4 cup rum
1/4 cup honey	

Place all in saucepan and bring to boil, then reduce heat and simmer for about 30 minutes. Cool. Pour over the cake and cut the Nut cake into diamond-shaped pieces for serving.

Peach Filo Pie

4 lbs. ripe peaches,
   peeled and sliced
Juice of 1/2 lemon
1 tsp. pumpkin pie
   spice
1 tsp. ground alspice
1 tsp. ground cloves

1 tsp. cornstarch
8 oz. can pineapple,
   with juice
5 Tbsps. honey
1 tsp. ground cinnamon
1 tsp. nutmeg
1 tsp. ground ginger

Butter a 13" x 9" baking pan. Place half of the Fillo dough in bottom of pan, brushing each sheet with butter, and overlapping the edges of the pan slightly.

Mix all the rest of the ingredients in a large bowl. Spoon the filling into the pan. Cover with the rest of the Fillo, buttering each sheet as you lay it in place. Tack in the ends. With a sharp knife, slit the top Fillo dough into diamond shapes.

Bake in a 375° oven for 25 to 30 minutes, until lightly brown.

Plum Cake

1 lb. plums, halved
1 orange peel, grated
1 lemon peel, grated
1/4 cup flour
1/2 cup cornstarch
2 Tbsps. Grand Marnier
Powdered sugar

1-1/2 cups sugar
1 cup butter
4 egg yolks
1 tsp. vanilla
1 Tbsp. baking powder
4 egg whites

Mix the plums with 1/2 cup of sugar and set aside. Cream butter and 1 cup of sugar. Separate the eggs and beat the four yolks into the butter one at a time. Stir in the grated lemon and orange peel and the vanilla.

In a separate bowl, combine the flour, cornstarch and baking powder. Fold this into the egg mixture.

Beat the egg whites until stiff. Fold in with the rest of the batter. Butter a 9-inch springform pan. Spoon half of the batter into the pan and bake in 350° oven for 10 minutes. Arrange plums cut side up on top of partially baked batter. Sprinkle Grand Marnier on top, along with the remaining batter. Bake another 55 to 60 minutes. Sprinkle with powdered sugar. Cool for at least an hour before serving.

Peanut Butter Cheesecake

1-1/4 cups graham
  cracker crumbs
1 lb. softened cream cheese
1 cup creamy peanut butter
1-1/2 cups sugar
Juice of 1/2 lemon
1/2 cup chopped walnuts

1/3 cup melted butter
1/4 cup sugar
6 eggs
1/2 cup sour cream
1 cup semisweet
  chocolate chips

Preheat oven to 350°.

Combine the graham crackers, butter, 1/2 cup of the sugar and the walnuts. Process until in crumbs. Butter a 9" springform pan. Press mixture onto the sides and bottom of the pan.

Combine the cream cheese, peanut butter, eggs, sour cream, 1-1/2 cups of sugar and lemon juice in a mixer or food processor until smooth. Add the chocolate chips, blending gently.

Spoon this mixture into the pie crust. Bake for an hour and 20 minutes.

Topping

3/4 cup semisweet
  chocolate chips, melted

1 cup sour cream
1/2 cup sugar

Blend the ingredients well. Cool the cheesecake for 15 to 20 minutes before you spread the topping on. After topping has been applied, bake for 10 more minutes. Makes 8 servings.

Cherry Cheesecake

1 cup graham cracker crumbs
1/2 cup finely chopped walnuts
1-1/2 lbs. cream cheese
2 cups sour cream
2 tsp. vanilla extract
10 oz. of cherry pie filling

10 oz. sweet black cherries
1/3 cup melted butter
1/4 cup sugar
1-1/2 more cups of sugar
6 eggs
2 Tbsps. cornstarch
1 Tbsp. lemon juice
2 Tbsps. grated orange peel
1 tsp. lemon juice

Preheat oven to 350°.

Mix graham crackers, nuts, butter and 1/4 cup of sugar. Press mixture firmly against the bottom and about 2-inches up the sides of a 9" springform pan. Beat cream cheese at medium speed until smooth. Beat 1-1/2 cups sugar in slowly. Then beat in the eggs, sour cream, cornstarch, vanilla extract and lemon juice. Spoon mixture into the crust and bake 1 hour-10 minutes, until brown. Turn off oven and leave cake in for another 20 minutes. Then cover and refrigerate 5-6 hours.

Remove from the pan and place on a serving plate. Mix the cherries, orange peel and lemon juice. Spoon this over the cheesecake and serve.

Brandy Pie

1-1/2 cups chocolate wafer crumbs
1 envelope unflavored gelatin
1/4 cup brandy
1/4 cup cream de cacao

1/4 cup sugar
1/2 cup melted butter
1/2 cup cold water
2/3 cups sugar
3 egg yolks
3 egg whites

Combine wafer crumbs, 1/4 cup of the sugar and the butter to make the pie crust. Press on sides and bottom of the 10" pie plate. Bake the crust for 10 minutes at 350°.

Mix the gelatin and cold water in a saucepan. Stir in the egg yolks and 1/3 cup sugar, then cook over low heat until smooth. Remove from heat. Stir in the brandy and cream de cacao and chill for about 1 hour. Beat egg whites until foamy. Beat 1/3 cup sugar into the egg whites. Stir and add to the gelatin mixture. Pour the filling into the crust. Garnish top with shaved chocolate. Chill for 3 to 4 hours and serve.

Peanut Butter Pie

3/4 stick butter, melted, cooled
2/3 cups graham cracker crumbs
1 cup confectioner's sugar
1 cup creamy peanut butter
1-1/2 cups whipping cream
4 Tbsps. chopped peanuts
3/4 cup sugar
4 oz. cream cheese
1/4 cup milk
1 tsp. vanilla
2 Tbsps. lemon juice

Mix butter, sugar and graham cracker crumbs well. Press in a 9" pie plate. Bake in a 425° oven for 10 minutes.

Cream together the cream cheese and confectioner's sugar. Beat in the milk, peanut butter, vanilla and lemon juice. Beat the whipping cream and fold it into the peanut butter mixture and mix well. Spoon filling into the pie shell.

Sprinkle the chopped peanuts over the top, cover, and chill overnight before serving.

Pie Crust

1 lb. pastry flour
2 Tbsps. non fat dry milk
1 tsp. white vinegar
1/2 cup ice cold water
1 egg yolk
1/4 lb. butter
1/4 lb. shortening
1 Tbsp. sugar
1 Tbsp. vegetable oil

Mix all ingredients except the water thoroughly. Then add the water slowly and mix to form a ball. Do not knead.

Harvest Pie

3 cups peeled apple slices
2 cups peeled pear slices
1 Tbsp. lemon juice
1/2 tsp. cinnamon
Pastry for 2 pie crusts
1-1/2 cups seedless grapes
1 tsp. lemon peel
1/2 cup sugar
2 Tbsps. flour
1/2 tsp. nutmeg

Combine ingredients for filling well. Divide pastry in half. Trim to fit 9" pie plate, overlapping slightly. Spoon in filling. Roll out remaining pastry, cut into 1/2" strips. Form a lattice top for the pie. Press strips to edges of bottom crust. Fold crust over strips to form a rim. Bake at 350° for about 60 minutes.

Rum Apple Pie

One 9" pie crust
2-1/2 lbs. apples, peeled,
  cored and sliced
1/2 cup quick rolled oats
3/4 cup pecans, chopped
1/2 cup melted butter

1 cup brown sugar
1/4 cup cornstarch
3 Tbsps. dark rum
1 tsp. cinnamon
1 more cup brown sugar
1/2 cup flour

Line a 9" pie plate with pie crust. Make a few holes in the bottom of the crust.

Combine apples, 1 cup of the brown sugar, cornstarch, rum and cinnamon. Spoon mixture into the pie shell.

Then mix together well the rolled oats, the other cup of brown sugar, the pecans, flour and melted butter. Sprinkle this over the apple mixture.

Bake in a preheated 350° oven for about 50 minutes.

Grand Marnier Pudding

1-1/2 cups Amaretto cookies,
  ground up
1-1/2 lbs. softened cream
  cheese
2 Tbsps. Grand Marnier

3 Tbsps. espresso coffee
1 cup sugar
2 eggs
1 Tbsp. rum

Soak cookies in espresso coffee for a few minutes. Add the rest of the ingredients to the cookies, blending until smooth. Spoon into serving glasses. Refrigerate for at least 2 hours. Makes about 8 servings.

"Nick cooks with Love and imagination. And all that he cooks is spiced with pride."

**Valjean and Brad
Syckes**

Papaya Parfaits

1-1/2 cups ginger snap
  cookie crumbs
3 Tbsps. cornstarch
1 Tbsp. grated orange peel
3 Tbsps. Grand Marnier
2 Tbsps. lemon juice
1/2 cup more of sugar

1/4 cup melted butter
1/2 cup sugar
2 cups milk
1 Tbsp. chopped ginger
1/2 cup extra butter
2 papayas
Whipping cream

Combine the cookie crumbs with 1/4 cup of melted butter.

In a separate saucepan, cook the milk, ginger, orange peel, cornstarch and 1/2 cup of sugar over medium heat until the mixture thickens. Remove from the stove. Add the extra 1/2 cup butter and the Grand Marnier and chill.

Slice eight pieces of the papaya fruit to use later as a garnish. Chop the rest of the papaya into cubes about 3/4" in size. Toss together the papaya cubes, lemon juice and the extra 1/2 cup of sugar.

In tall glasses, layer:
  chopped papaya
  cream mixture
  ginger crumbs

Repeat the layers until each glass is nearly full. Top with whipped cream and garnish with the 8 papaya slices.

Chocolate Souffle

5 egg yolks
1 cup flour
2 oz. unsweetened chocolate,
  melted
8 egg whites
Whipping cream

1/2 cups sugar
1 tsp. vanilla
2 cups milk
1/4 cup more sugar
Powdered sugar

Beat egg yolks, 1/2 cup sugar and vanilla until fluffy. Gradually beat in flour. Bring milk to boil in saucepan, add egg mixture, whisking until smooth. Add chocolate and extra 1/4 cup sugar, then cool. Beat egg whites until stiff. Spoon into a 12" buttered and sugared souffle dish. Bake at 350° for one hour. Dust with powdered sugar and top with whipping cream.

Maple Mousse

1 cup maple syrup
2 tsp. maple extract
2 Tbsps. unflavored gelatin
4 egg whites, beaten
1 extra cup whipping cream
3 Tbsps. dark rum
1 tsp. vanilla extract
2 more egg yolks
1/4 cup sugar

4 egg yolks
1/2 cup brown sugar
1/2 cup cold water
2 cups whipping cream
1 tsp. vanilla
1 cup milk
2 Tbsps. cornstarch
1 extra tsp. vanilla

Cook maple syrup and maple extract, 4 egg yolks and the brown sugar in a double pan; boil for about 10 minutes.

Mix the gelatin in cold water, add to the maple syrup and stir well. Mix 2 cups of the whipping cream, 1 teaspoon of vanilla and 4 egg whites (beaten until stiff), and fold this into the gelatin/maple mixture. Fill serving glasses 3/4 full of this mix, and refrigerate for about 5 hours.

In a double pan, boil the other cup of whipping cream, the milk, rum and vanilla extract. Bring to a gentle boil.

In a separate bowl, mix the cornstarch, 1 teaspoon of vanilla, 2 egg yolks and the granulated sugar. Add the cream mixture to this slowly, stirring constantly. Then cook this sauce for five more minutes and remove from heat. When cool, spoon this sauce over the refrigerated maple mousse and serve.

Strawberry Fritters

Oil for frying (heat
  to 400°)
Pancake mix (see page 1)

Whole strawberries
Powdered sugar

Add strawberries to the pancake batter and stir until all berries are coated on all sides. Drop coated strawberries into the oil and fry until light brown. Sprinkle each with a light dusting of powdered sugar before serving.

Fried Milk

1/2 cup coconut milk
1 cup sugar
2 cups water
1-1/2 Tbsps. baking powder
1-1/2 cups flour
1-1/2 cups more of water
Powdered sugar

3/4 cup half and half
6 Tbsps. cornstarch
1/4 tsp. butter
Oil for frying
3 Tbsps. oil
1 egg, beaten

Combine coconut milk and half and half in a pan. Add the cornstarch, stir, then add the sugar, 2 cups of water and the butter. Heat until mixture boils and begins to thicken. Pour into a pan, chill to set.

When firm, cut mixture into small pieces. Heat the oil for frying in a skillet. Combine the flour, baking powder, 3 tablespoons of oil, 1-1/2 cups extra water and the beaten egg. Beat until smooth.

Dip pieces of chilled milk mix into the batter. Fry each piece until golden brown, or for about 3 minutes. Sprinkle with powdered sugar before serving.

Peanut Butter Brownies

1/2 cup butter, softened
1/2 cup peanut butter
1/2 cup quick oats
1 tsp. baking soda
1/2 cup chopped nuts
1/3 cup more peanut butter
3 Tbsps. cocoa powder

1/2 cup sugar
1/2 cup brown sugar
2 eggs
1 cup flour
1/4 tsp. salt
1-1/2 cups powdered sugar
1/4 cup milk
3 Tbps. more milk

Mix well the sugar, brown sugar, eggs, butter and 1/2 cup of peanut butter. Combine separately the flour, oats, baking soda, salt and nuts, and mix with the rest of the ingredients. Spoon into a 13" x 9" greased pan. Bake at 350° for 20 minutes and then cool. Mix powdered sugar, 1/3 cup peanut butter and mix well. Remove 1/3 cup of the mix and put aside. Spread remaining frosting on top of brownies. Mix the removed frosting with cocoa powder and 3 tablespoons of milk. Swirl in a marble effect on top of other frosting. About 28 servings.

Cheesecake Brownies

4 oz. unsweetened butter	1 cup sugar
2 oz. unsweetened chocolate	1/4 tsp. salt
1/2 tsp. vanilla extract	2 eggs
1 cup chopped pecans	1/2 cup flour
1/2 cup shredded coconut	8 oz. cream cheese
2 Tbsps. cocoa powder	1/2 cup more of sugar
1/2 tsp. vanilla extract	2 more eggs
1/2 tsp. almond extract	1 more Tbsp. flour

Butter a 9" x 9" pan. Melt 4 ounces of butter and the unsweetened chocolate over low heat. Stir in a cup of sugar, the salt and vanilla extract. Remove from heat and stir in 2 eggs, then add 1/2 cup flour, the pecans and coconut and stir well.

Turn the batter into the buttered pan, smooth the top and set aside.

Beat the cream cheese, 1/2 cup sugar, cocoa powder and 1/2 teaspoon of the vanilla extract and the almond extract until smooth. Add 2 more eggs and another tablespoon of flour and mix thoroughly. Pour this cream sauce over the brownie layer and smooth the top.

Insert the handle of a teaspoon in one of the corners of the cake, almost to the bottom. Cut through the batter in a wide zig-zag pattern, and again smooth the top.

Bake in a 350° oven for about 40 minutes. Remove and then freeze brownies for about 1 hour, until firm. Cut into squares and serve.

Chocolate Chip Cookies

3/4 cup brown sugar	1/2 cup butter
3/4 cup sugar	1/2 cup margarine
2 tsps. vanilla	2 eggs
1-1/2 cups chopped walnuts	3 cups flour
3-1/2 cups chocolate chips	1/2 tsp. soda
	1/2 tsp. salt

Mix butter, margarine, sugar, eggs and vanilla well. Combine flour, soda, salt, nuts and chips. Combine two mixes and form into small balls. Place on a greased sheet and bake in a 325° oven for about 15 to 20 minutes.

Oatmeal Raisin Cookies

1 cup margarine	1 cup butter
1 cup granulated sugar	1 cup brown sugar
2 eggs	1 Tbsp. molasses
2-1/2 cups quick oats	2-1/2 cups flour
1-1/2 cups chopped walnuts	2 tsp. soda
1 tsp. salt	2 tsp. cinnamon
1-1/2 cups raisins	

Combine butter, margarine, sugar, eggs and molasses. Mix thoroughly. Put the flour, oats, soda, cinnamon, salt, raisins and chopped walnuts in a separate bowl and mix well, then add to the first set of ingredients. Mix completely, then form into small balls. Place in greased pans and bake in a 325° oven for about 15 to 20 minutes.

Oatmeal Orange Cookies

3/4 cup butter	1 cup sugar
1 tsp. orange extract	1 egg
1/8 cup molasses	1-1/2 cups flour
1 tsp. grated orange peel	1 tsp. soda
1/4 tsp. salt	1 tsp. cinnamon
1 can quick oats	1 tsp. ginger
2/3 cup raisins	

Completely mix the butter, sugar, egg, orange extract and molasses. Separately, combine the other ingredients, then put the two mixtures together and combine thoroughly.

Form into small balls. Place on a greased baking sheet and bake in a 325° for about 15 to 20 minutes.

Spice Cookies

1/8 cup Worchestershire sauce 3/4 cup butter
1 cup dark brown sugar 1 egg
1/8 cup molasses 2-1/4 cups flour
1-1/2 tsp. cinnamon 2 tsp. soda
1/2 tsp. ground ginger 1/2 tsp. ground alspice
1/4 tsp. salt 1/2 tsp. ground cloves

Mix butter, sugar, egg, molasses and Worchestershire sauce well together. Combine the other ingredients and blend with the first mixture thoroughly. Refrigerate for 15 minutes, then form into small balls. Bake on an ungreased sheet at 350° for about 10 to 15 minutes.

Peanut Butter Cookies

1/2 cup margarine 1/2 cup butter
1 cup crunchy peanut butter 1 cup brown sugar
1 tsp. baking powder 2 eggs
1 tsp. baking soda 2-1/2 cups flour
1/4 tsp. salt 1 cup sugar

Mix margarine, butter, peanut butter, sugar and eggs well. Combine with other ingredients and mix thoroughly. Form into small balls and place in greased pans. Bake at 325° for about 15 to 20 minutes.

Almond Cookies

1/2 lb. sweet butter, softened	1/2 cup powdered sugar
1 Tbsp. brandy	1 egg yolk
1/2 tsp. vanilla extract	2-1/2 cups flour, sifted
1/2 tsp. almond extract	1/2 cup chopped almonds

Whip butter for about 20 minutes, until fluffy. Add sugar, egg yolk, brandy, and the vanilla and almond extract and whip for a few more minutes, until all is well mixed.

Add the flour and almonds, mixing until dough is formed.

Make a ball a little bigger than a walnut, roll it into an egg shape, place it on a baking sheet, and press down to flatten. Place a whole clove in the middle of the cookie.

Repeat until dough is used up. Bake at 350° for about 20 to 25 minutes. Dust powdered sugar on the top of each cookie when done. Makes about 36 to 40 cookies.

Chocolate Bread

3 packages of dry yeast	1/2 cup warm water
4 more cups of warm water	1 tsp. sugar
2 Tbsps. melted butter	1 egg
1/3 cup additional sugar	1 Tbsp. salt
1 cup unsweetened cocoa	12 cups flour
1 lb. semi-sweet chocolate chips	

Combine yeast with 1/2 cup of warm water and a teaspoon of sugar. Let sit for 5 minutes.

Add the extra warm water and sugar, the egg, melted butter and salt to the yeast, and mix well. Add the flour, cocoa and the chocolate chips and knead until dough is elastic.

Place in a greased bowl. Cover with a cloth and let dough rise until it approximately doubles in size, or for about 1 hour.

Divide into 8 pieces. Shape each piece into a loaf or round. Place these on a greased baking sheet. Cover again and let rise until doubled in size again. Uncover and bake in a 375° oven for 35 to 40 minutes.

Seed Bread

1/2 cup warm water	3 packages of dry yeast
1-3/4 cup more of warm water	1-1/2 Tbsps. sugar
3 cups unbleached flour	1 cup warm milk
3 cups whole wheat flour	2 Tbsps. vegetable oil
1 cup unprocessed bran	1 tsp. salt
1/2 cup golden raisins	1 egg
1/2 cup chopped walnuts	1/2 cup honey
1/2 cup poppy seeds	1/2 cup sunflower seeds
1 cup corn meal	1 egg
1 egg white	1/2 cup honey
1 extra tsp. water	

Dissolve yeast in 1/2 cup of warm water with the sugar. Let sit for 5 minutes. Add the extra water, flour and warm milk to the yeast, cover, set in a warm place until dough doubles in size. Add the vegetable oil, salt, egg and honey and knead.

Add the cornmeal, rye flour, whole wheat flour, and bran. Knead some more. If too sticky, add more white flour.

Add the raisins, walnuts, sunflower seeds and poppy seeds. Mix well.

Place in a greased bowl and cover. Let rise until double in size.

Divide dough into 3 pieces. Place in greased loaf pans (9" x 4"), let rise almost to the top of the pan. Bake in a 350° oven for 55 to 60 minutes.

When done, combine egg white and 1 teaspoon of water and use this to brush the top of each loaf.

Strawberry Bread

1 tsp. almond extract
2 eggs, separated
1 tsp. baking powder
1-1/2 cups strawberries,
    chopped

1/2 tsp. salt
1/2 cup butter
1 cup sugar
2 cups flour
1 tsp. soda

Cream butter, sugar and almond extract together in a large bowl. Beat in the yolks of the two eggs, one at a time. Add the flour, baking powder, soda and salt and mix well. Add the strawberries. Beat the 2 egg whites until stiff, and add them to the mixture.

Line a 9" x 5" pan with greased waxed paper. Pour the batter into the pan and bake in a 350° oven for about 1 hour. Allow to cool about 20 minutes before removing the bread from the pan. Makes one loaf.

Fennel Bread

1 package dry yeast
1/2 cup of warm water
2 tsps. fennel seeds
4 cups unbleached flour
2 more tsps. fennel seeds

1 tsp. sugar
1/2 cup warm water
2 tsps. salt
2 Tbsps. melted butter
1 egg
1 more tsp. sugar

Mix the yeast, a teaspoon of sugar and 1/2 cup of the warm water, and let stand for 5 minutes. Add the rest of the warm water, the salt, 2 teaspoons of the fennel seeds and the melted butter to the yeast and mix well for about 5 minutes. Add the flour and mix until the dough is stiff.

Knead on a floured surface for 6 to 8 minutes, adding more flour if necessary. Place the dough in a greased bowl. Let it rise, covered with a cloth, until doubled in size. Knead again, shape into a loaf. Place on a baking sheet and cover. Let it rise about 1 hour in a warm place. Slice across the top of the loaf in cuts about 1/2" deep. Beat together the egg, another teaspoon of sugar and 2 more teaspoons of fennel seeds and use this to brush the top of the loaf. Bake in a 375° oven 30 to 35 minutes.

Lemon Bread

1/2 cup margarine	1 cup sugar
1-1/4 cups unbleached flour	2 eggs, beaten
3/4 cup grated walnuts	1/2 cup milk
1/4 tsp. salt	1 tsp. baking powder
3 tsp. grated lemon rind	Juice of 1 lemon
1/4 cup more of sugar	

Cream together margarine and 1 cup of sugar. Mix in the beaten egg and milk, then stir in the flour, baking powder and salt. Also stir in the walnuts and lemon rind.

Butter a 9" x 5" loaf pan and pour batter into it. Bake in a 350° oven for about 1 hour. Remove from oven and pierce holes on top of the loaf. Combine lemon juice and 1/4 cup of sugar and use as a glaze, pouring over the top of the bread.

Herb Bread

2 packages dry yeast	1/2 tsp. rosemary chopped
2 Tbsps. oil	cups warm milk
6 cups unbleached flour	2 Tbsps. sugar
1/2 tsp. crumbled tarragon	1/2 tsp. salt
leaves	1/2 tsp. thyme, crumbled

Dissolve yeast in warm milk. Stir sugar and oil into the yeast. Mix together the flour, salt, thyme, tarragon and rosemary, and add this to the yeast mixture. Knead until smooth and elastic.

Place in a greased bowl. Cover. Let rise until double in size, or for about 1 hour. Divide into 3 pieces, shaping each into a loaf. Place in 7-1/2" x 3-1/2" loaf pans and cover. Again let rise until double in size.

Brush top with milk and about 1 tablespoon of fennel seeds. Bake in a 375° oven about 40 to 45 minutes.

"Eating at Nick's spoils you. He becomes the 'yardstick' against which all other restaurants are measured.
"Nick puts a lot of love into every dish."

Ralph Martini, Phoenix

Sausage Bread

1 cup raisins	1-1/2 cups brown sugar
1 lb. mild sausages, chopped	1-1/2 cups sugar
1 cup pecans, chopped	2 eggs
1 tsp. ginger	3 cups flour
1 tsp. pumpkin pie spice	1 tsp. baking powder
1 cup cold coffee	1 tsp. baking soda

Simmer raisins for 5 minutes, and drain. Mix all the ingredients with the raisins, adding the cold coffee and baking soda last. Grease and flour a 9" tube pan and spoon mixture into it. Bake in a 350° oven for about 1-1/2 hours.

12   Small Town U.S.A   Summer 1986

From Soccer Star to Entrepreneur

by Brad Steiger

Do you want to hear a genuine, old-fashioned American success story? Then come along to the Golden Pizzeria at 5204 East McDowell in Phoenix, Arizona. But come prepared to stand in line, for folks drive from as far away as Texas to eat a meal prepared by Nick Ligidakis.

What's the secret to the men and women patiently standing outside the door of the Golden Pizzeria? Why would some of these people drive for hours for the express privilege of waiting their turn to sample one of Nick's meals?

In a softly accented voice, Nick explains: "I make everything for each meal after the order has been placed. Nothing is processed or waiting in the refrigerator. And every one of my recipes is original. I have created each one of them."

Pretty good for an athlete who never had fixed more than scrambled eggs and toast before he came to the United States.

Let us travel back a few years. Nick Ligidakis was one of Greece's premier soccer stars. Hailing from the small town

Success

Right, that is, if the big-time promoters hadn't run out of money a few weeks after they had passed under the Statue of Liberty's torch. So there Nick was, stranded in Chicago. His fraction of the fabulous salary that he had been promised was so small that no one had to worry about this Greek bearing gifts.

Some of his desperate teammates wired home to Greece for money to fly back to familiar soccer fields, but Nick decided to test the American Dream Machine for himself.

A small restaurant caught his attention. Its owners, a married couple, wanted to sell. Nick had probably no more than pocket change, but he walked into the place and told the man and his wife that he would pay them what they asked. He was an honest, hard-working man, and he would make good the asking price if they would give him a chance.

When they responded to his sincere and earnest manner by accepting his terms, Nick literally moved into the restaurant and began to make it his total universe.

"I had no other place to stay," he laughs. "I had no apartment, no car. But now I had the Golden Pizzaria. I slept on an air mattress in the back. I worked from eight in the morning until two the next morning, seven days a week, for 18 months without a single day off."

Commitment. Discipline. Hard work. It paid off. Once you have savored the masterful Southern European cooking — whether you have eaten a complete meal, ordered a pizza or had one of those incredible submarine sandwiches — you have

Pepper Cheese Bread

1 package yeast
1-1/2 cups more of warm
  water
2 Tbsps. melted butter
5 Tbsps. sugar
1 tsp. salt
5-1/2 cups flour

1 cup grated sharp cheese
1/4 cup warm water
1 tsp. sugar
1 egg
1/2 cup milk
1 tsp. black pepper
1/2 tsp. basil

Dissolve yeast and 1 teaspoon of sugar in 1/4 cup of warm water. Let stand for 5 minutes. Add the rest of warm water, melted butter, egg and milk and mix well. Then add the extra 5 tablespoons of sugar, salt, pepper, basil and flour and mix thoroughly until soft and elastic. Place dough in a greased bowl and cover. Let rise for 1 hour. Then knead the grated sharp cheese into the dough.

Place into two 9" x 3" loaf pans. Brush melted butter on top of the loaves and let rise until double in size, for about one and one-half hours. Bake in a 350° oven for 50 to 55 minutes.

Sour Cream Bread

1 pack yeast
2 Tbsps. melted butter
2 Tbsps. sugar
1 cup sour cream
1/4 cup grated Parmesan
  cheese
Melted butter
1 egg white

1/4 cup warm water
1 egg
1 tsp. salt
1 tsp. dill weed
1 cup unbleached flour
1-1/4 cups rye flour
1 more Tbsp. water

Dissolve yeast in 1/4 cup warm water. Mix egg, 2 tablespoons of melted butter, sugar, salt, dill weed and sour cream with yeast and beat for about 2 to 3 minutes.

Stir in the flour and grated Parmesan. If the dough is not stiff, add more rye flour. Knead until smooth and elastic. Place in a greased bowl, cover, let rise until double in size — for about 1-1/2 hours. Shape into a ball and place in an 8" round pan. Brush with melted butter and let rise again until double. Mix egg white with 1 tablespoon of water and use this to brush the top of the loaf, and then bake in a 375° oven for about 40 minutes. Makes 1 round loaf.

Potato Bread

1 package dry yeast	1/2 cup warm water
3/4 cup more warm water	3 Tbsps. flour
1 tsp. caraway seeds	1 tsp. salt
4 cups unbleached flour	1/2 cup mashed potatoes

Dissolves yeast with 3 tablespoons of flour in 1/2 cup of warm water. Let stand for 1/2 hour. The stir in the rest of the warm water, the salt and caraway seeds. Slowly add the mashed potatoes and flour, mixing until dough is elastic. Knead for about 10 minutes.

Add flour to a greased bowl. Place dough in the bowl, cover, and let rise until double in size — or for about 1/2 hour.

Put dough into a round pan, or form into a loaf. Brush with water and cut a 1/4" deep cross in the top. Bake in a 375° oven for one hour and 15 minutes.

What better place to bring a date than Golden Cuisine?

9

A Special "Bonus" From Nick

So many people have been asking me: "When are you going to make something with a lot of chocolate?"
Well, here it is . . . a dessert with a lot of chocolate. With this one, my friends, you are in Chocolate Heaven!

Sweet Chocolate Death

Meringue

2 Tbsps. unsweetened cocoa   4 egg whites
3/4 cup sugar

Heat the egg whites and sugar in a double boiler, beating until just warm. Remove from heat, beat at medium speed for 12 to 14 minutes, and add the cocoa. Mix well. Butter a 9" pan, line it with paper then butter it again. Bake meringue in a 200° oven for one and one-half hours, remove and cool.

Genoise

3/4 cup sugar   5 egg yolks
4 Tbsps. unsalted butter   5 eggs
4 Tbsps. unsweetened cocoa   1 cup cake flour

Heat the sugar and eggs in a double boiler until just warm. Remove from heat and beat at high speed for 10 to 12 minutes. Add the butter, cocoa and flour, mixing well. Pour into a 9-inch buttered and floured springform pan. Bake at 350° for 45 minutes, remove from oven. Cool completely, then slice into layers about one-half inch thick.

Chocolate Mousse Filling

Melt 1-1/4 pound of bittersweet chocolate in a double boiler. After the chocolate has cooled, beat in 7 egg yolks, one at a time. Beat the 8 egg whites until stiff, then add them to the chocolate. Add 1/2 cup of sugar to the mixture, mix until smooth.

Chocolate Icing

Heat 12 ounces of semisweet chocolate and 1-2/3 cups of whipping cream in a double boiler. Blend well until smooth.

Assembling

Place the meringue in the bottom of a 9-inch springform pan. Cover with one-half of the icing and with one layer of the Genoise. Pour one-half of the Mousse on top of the Genoise, then place the other slice of the Genoise on the Mousse and cover both with the rest of the Mousse.

Refrigerate for about four hours. Before serving, cover the entire cake with the rest of the icing and with sliced blanced almonds.

A large dinner party of enthusiastic Golden Cuisine fans who are happily introducing the delights of Nick's cooking to their friends.

Because so many of you have been trying to guess the ingredients of another favorite treat, I have also decided to share the recipe for:

Spearmint Cheesecake

Crust

1-1/4 cup chocolate
  wafer crumbs
1/3 cup melted, unsalted
  butter

1/2 cup sugar

Mix well and press against the bottom and sides of a lightly buttered 9-inch springform pan.

Filling

2-1/2 lbs. cream cheese
1/4 cup milk
5 oz. semisweet chocolate
5 oz. mint chocolate chips
2 Tbsps. green creme
  de menthe

1-1/2 cups sugar
5 eggs
2 tsp. mint extract
2 Tbsps. flour

Beat the cream cheese until smooth. Add the sugar and beat until smooth. Melt the chocolate in a double boiler. Add the rest of the ingredients, beat until smooth. Pour the mixture over the crust, then bake in a 350° oven for about one hour.

Topping

1/2 cup semisweet chocolate
1/2 cup chocolate mint chips

1 cup sour cream
1/2 cup sugar

Melt the semisweet chocolate and the chocolate mint chips in a double boiler. Add the sour cream and sugar. Turn off the oven and spread the topping on top of the cake and leave it inside the oven for another half-hour. Cover the cake and refrigerate for five to six hours before serving.

For Thanksgiving 1986, Nick and Karen donated 250 turkey dinners to the Central Arizona Shelter Services. Mary Orton, Executive Director of the shelter, accepted the meals and saw to their distribution.

"I don't feel comfortable sitting at a big table filled with food, knowing that there are other people starving," Nick commented. "So I do something that makes me happy — I give some food to those who really need to eat.

"I wish that more people would feel motivated to do this kind of thing on this special day. And more than on just that one day, I wish people would always show compassion for those less fortunate."

Index to
Nick's Creative Cooking Made Easy

A

Agnolotti, 56
Agnolotti Romana, 66
Almond Cookies 115
Antipasto, 42

Appetizers and Creations, 11

Apricot Hens, 73
Artichoke (Fried Hearts), 22
Artichoke Sole, 84
Asparagus in Filo, 19
Asparagus Spears, 16
Avocado Tarama, 21

B

Baklava, 102
Barbeque Sauce, 96
Bean Soup, 32
B-B-Q Beef Sandwich, 47
Bleu Roast Beef Sandwich, 47
Brandy Pie, 106
Broccoli Melt, 14

BROTH

Beef, 26

INDEX *(Continued)*

BROTH *(Continued)*

Chicken, 25
Fish, 26
Lamb, 27
Vegetable, 25

BURGERS

Athenian, 49
Bacon, 48
Californian, 48
Hawaiian, 48
Italian, 48
Western, 48

C

Cabbage Soup, 31
Calamari Capellini, 80
Calamari Provencale, 85

CALZONE

Cheese, 51
Meatball or Sausage, 52
Vegetable, 51

Cappaletti, 56
Capellini Tonato, 66
Cassoulet, 35
Cauliflower Roquefort Soup, 28
Cheese Triangles, 20
Cheesecake Brownies, 112

INDEX *(Continued)*

C *(Continued)*

Cherry Cheesecake, 106

CHICKEN

Beggar's, 71
Bleu, 68
Kapama, 69
Lemony, 67
Palm, 67
Picata, 70
Plaka, 68

Chicken Fritters, 24
Chocolate Bread, 115
Chocolate Chip Cookies, 112
Chocolate Souffle, 109
Cocktail Sauce, 97
Cornish Hens Spinaci, 72
Crab Avocado Salad, 41

CROISSANTS

Avocado, 50
Francheese, 50
Shrimp-Pineapple, 50

D

Desserts and Breads, 102

Dough (Pizza), 53

INDEX *(Continued)*

E

EGG

Baked (Sandwich), 46
Lemon Soup, 26
Pasta, 55

EGGPLANT

Baked (Soup), 32
Dip, 98
Mousaka, 87
Parmigiana, 89
Ripieri, 17
Salad, 39
Stuffed, 87

Escargot, 17

F

Fennel Bread, 117
Feta Leaves, 19
Fettucini Formaggi, 60
Fish Roe Salad, 21
Fish Soup, 34
Fried Milk, 111
Fusilli Privavera, 65

G

Garden Soup, 29

INDEX *(Continued)*

G *(Continued)*

Garlic Toast, 23
Golden Salad, 40
Golden Steak Sandwich, 44
Grand Marnier Pudding, 108
Green Pasta, 55
Greek Salad, 37
Gyros, 75

H

Harvest Pie, 107
Herb Bread, 118

K

Kataifi, 103
Korinthian Sea Bass, 84

L

LAMB

Classic, 74
In Foil, 74
Roman, 75
Sliced (Salad), 41

Lemon Bread, 118
Lentil Soup, 33

INDEX *(Continued)*

L *(Continued)*

LINGUINI

Clam, 63
Pesce, 65

Lasagne Il Re, 61

M

Manicotti Marinara, 64
Maple Mousse, 110
Marinara Sauce, 97
Meat Balls, 99
Meat Ball Sandwich, 46
Meat Sauce, 93
Minestrone, 36
Monte Cristo, 45
Mostaccioli Primo, 63
Mozzarella (Sticks, fried), 15
Mushroom (Deep Fried), 12
Mustard Sauce, 97

N

Nut Cake, 103

O

Oatmeal Orange Cookies, 113
Oatmeal Raisin Cookies, 113

INDEX *(Continued)*

O *(Continued)*

ONIONS

Fried Hearts, 21
Rings, 23
Stuffed, 16

P

Papaya Parfaits, 109
Pasta Salad, 38
Peach Filo Pie, 104
Peanut Butter Brownies, 111
Peanut Butter Cookies, 114
Peanut Butter Cheesecake, 105
Peanut Butter Pie, 107
Pepper Cheese Bread, 120
Pepper Steak Sandwich, 43
Pepperoni Tirato, 22
Pesto Sauce, 96
Pie Crust, 107
Pizza, 53
Pizza Sauce, 92
Plum Cake, 104

Pocket-Roll Sandwiches and Croissants, 43

Potato Bread, 121
Potato Skins — Stuffed, 89
Potato Spinach Soup, 28
Provolone (Baked Soup), 30

INDEX *(Continued)*

R

Ravioli, 57
Ravioli Bolognese, 61
Red Pepper Soup, 30
Reuben Sandwich, 44
Rice Balls (Fried), 13
Rice Pilaf, 98
Rum Apple Pie, 108

S

Salads, 37

Sauces and Dressings, 92

Sausage Bread, 119
Sausage Sandwich, 47
Scallops (Marine), 81
Scallops Plaki, 80
Scrod Broccoli, 82
Seed Bread, 118

SHRIMP

Athena, 83
Balls, 24
Bay, Fried, 14
Coconut Fried, 83
Feta, 81
Pasta, 39

Smelts Milanese, 82

INDEX *(Continued)*

S *(Continued)*

Snails (Brochettes), 18

Soups, 25

Sour Cream Bread, 120
Spaghetti Carbonara, 59
Spearmint Cheesecake, 124
Spice Cookies, 114
Spinach Garlic Soup, 27
Spinach Triangles, 20

STEAK

Baby Corn, 78
Metaxa, 79
Peppery, 79
Stefado, 78

Strawberry Bread, 117
Strawberry Fritters, 110
Stuffed Shells Spinaci, 62
Sweet Chocolate Death, 122

T

Tarama Avocado Dip, 98
Tartar Sauce, 97
Tortellini, 57
Tortellini Prosciutto, 38
Tortellini Romanolla, 60
Tuna Melt, 45
Turkey Tostada, 73

INDEX *(Continued)*

V

Vegetable Soup (Baked), 31

W

Whole Wheat Crust (Pizza), 54

Y

Yogurt Dressing, 93

Z

ZUCCHINI

> Fried, 12
> Stuffed, 86
> Stuffed Flowers, 18

NOTES & PERSONAL RECIPES

NOTES & PERSONAL RECIPES

NOTES & PERSONAL RECIPES

NOTES & PERSONAL RECIPES

NOTES & PERSONAL RECIPES